THE ULTIMATE GUIDE TO
DINOSAURS

by Dougal Dixon
B.Sc. (HONS.), M.Sc.

C O N T E N T S

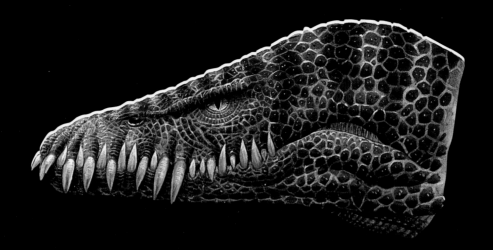

People have always been fascinated by dinosaurs! From the earliest discoveries of dinosaur bones in the mid-19th century, children and adults alike have wanted to read all about these giant creatures: where they lived, what they ate, what they looked like, and how they were eventually wiped out. This book provides a comprehensive look at the world of the dinosaurs, looking at them from both a historical and scientific viewpoint. *Read on to discover...*

INTRODUCTION

HISTORY OF PALAEONTOLOGY

For many hundreds of years, people were puzzled by massive bones found poking out from cliffs and beaches. But it was not until the 19th century that scientists began to try to work out what these fossils might actually mean. Today, paleontologists know that they were the bones of dinosaurs and have pieced together a strong picture of this ancient world. We now know that dinosaurs lived millions of years ago; and that there were many different types of these creatures. This book takes you through the history of dinosaur hunting, tells you how fossils are formed, and even find out how bones are discovered and excavated.

HERBIVORES & CARNIVORES, LAND, SEA & SKY

Certain types of dinosaurs are grouped together for easy reference. First you will meet the meat-eating "**carnivores**"—including the ferocious Tyrannosaurus (and his even-bigger brothers); next, the vegetarian "**herbivores**"—like the Sauropod with the long, long neck so he can reach the highest leaves! Following on, you will plunge into the watery depths with **dinosaurs from the sea**—and learn how these creatures' powerful bodies were so suitable for a life in the ocean. Lastly, you will encounter the prehistoric **beasts of the sky**—such as the brilliantly colored pterodactyl.

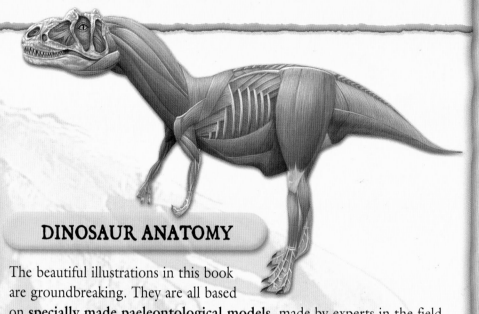

DINOSAUR ANATOMY

The beautiful illustrations in this book
are groundbreaking. They are all based
on **specially made paeleontological models**, made by experts in the field.
This means that the illustrations show not just the body shape, but also
skin texture, muscle formation and colorings.

NEW THEORIES

This book also takes an in-depth look at
different palaeontological theories, and
the **disagreements between experts.**
The book looks at recent feathered
dinosaur fossils, for example, and why
they have encouraged some paleontologists
to come up with bold theories about what
happened to the dinosaurs. While some still suggest the dinosaurs were
wiped out by a meteor storm, others are now saying that they never
really died at all, but developed into creatures with feathers. **This book
looks at the evidence and asks the reader to draw their own
conclusions from the wealth of information presented.**

IMPORTANT FINDS

Finally, this book contains
**significant recent fossil
finds,** from the prehistoric
birds and fish dug up in the
Solnofen Quarry to the
Chinese "Gang of Three," the feathered
dinosaurs that have caused so much debate.
Turn the page to find out about the
gripping world of the dinosaurs.

TIMELINE

4.6 BILLION YEARS AGO

Formation of the Earth

3.5–2.8 BILLION YEARS AGO

First life on Earth—algae

**1500–600 MILLION
YEARS AGO**

*First sea animals with shells
and skeletons*

500–450 MILLION YEARS AGO

First fish

420 MILLION YEARS AGO

First land animals—millipedes

375 MILLION YEARS AGO

First shark ancestors

350–300 MILLION YEARS AGO

*First amphibians,
primitive insects*

300–200 MILLION YEARS AGO

*First reptiles, winged insects,
cockroaches, bees, primitive
crocodiles and mammals.
FIRST DINOSAURS!*

200–20 MILLION YEARS AGO

*Dinosaurs disappear and
modern animal life begins
to flourish*

**20–2 MILLION
YEARS AGO**

*First chimpanzees and
earliest humans*

1.6–2 MILLION YEARS AGO

Mammoths disappear

5–0 MILLION YEARS AGO

First modern humans

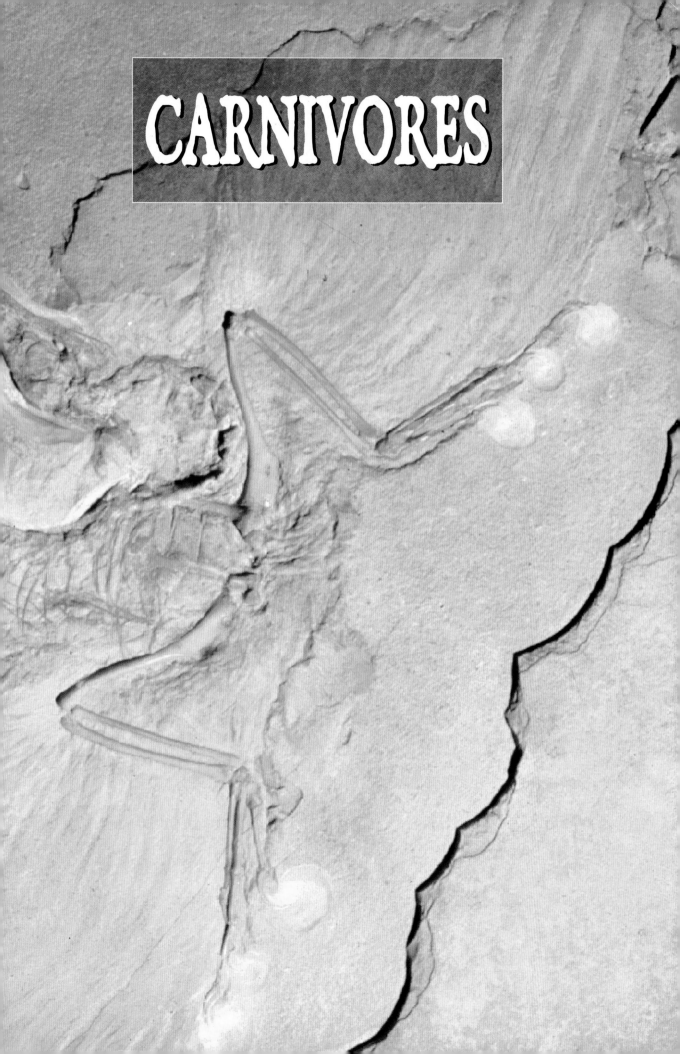

CARNIVORES

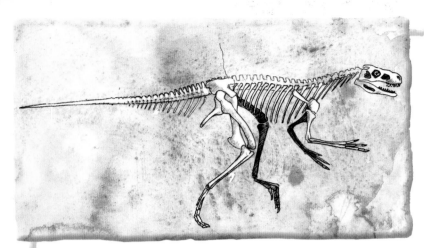

POWERFUL LEGS

A meat-eating dinosaur, *Herrerasaurus* walked on strong hind legs, with its teeth and the claws on its arms held out to the front where they could do most damage. The back was held horizontally and the body was balanced by a long tail. This set the pattern for all meat-eating dinosaurs to come.

BEFORE THE DINOSAURS

During the Permian period, the main plant-eating animals of the time were mammal-like reptiles. They had teeth like mammals, and some were even hairy. The biggest were built like hippopotami, such as the broad-headed *Moschops* shown here. At the same time as the first dinosaurs developed, the first mammals developed too. Descended from the mammal-like reptiles, they were small and furry and bore live young. If the dinosaurs had not come to prominence, the mammals may well have taken over. Instead, they had to wait 160 million years before they became the dominent form of life on Earth.

EORAPTOR

Eoraptor was about the size of a fox and, like all the dinosaurs to follow, walked on legs that were held straight under the body. This made it a much faster animal than the other reptiles that walked on legs sprawled out to the side of their bodies.

TIGER-SIZED

Herrerasaurus was a much bigger animal than *Eoraptor*, about the size of a tiger. One of the first dinosaurs, it was a primitive theropod, the dinosaur group that includes all the meat-eaters. Adults could reach a length of 10 feet (3 m). The skeleton of a *Herrerasaurus* was found in Argentina, in South America.

8

WHERE DID THEY COME FROM?

Dinosaurs! The most famous of all extinct animals, the whale-sized reptiles that dominated the Earth for about 160 million years. Reptiles developed during the Carboniferous period, about 350 million years ago, and flourished during the succeeding Permian, Triassic, Jurassic and Cretaceous periods. During this Age of Reptiles there were land-living reptiles, swimming reptiles, flying reptiles—reptiles of all kinds in every environment. Some were herbivores (plant-eaters), some carnivores (meat-eaters) and others omnivores (both plant and meat-eaters). At the end of the Cretaceous era, about 65 million years ago, all the big reptiles died out and mammals took over. The Age of Reptiles was well under way before the first dinosaurs appeared around the end of the Triassic period, 225 million years ago.

EORAPTOR SKULL

An x-ray photograph of *Eoraptor's* skull shows how its lightweight skull was made up of thin struts of bone. The dinosaur's light bone structure enabled it to move fast. The skulls of most subsequent meat-eating dinosaurs were built like this.

RAUISUCHIAN

Before the dinosaurs came along, the biggest of the hunters were a group of land-living crocodile relatives called rauisuchians. They had big heads and many sharp teeth and, although they were slow-moving, were faster than the plant-eating reptiles of the time.

CARBONIFEROUS 360-286 MYA	PERMIAN 286-248 MYA	TRIASSIC 245-208 MYA	EARLY/MID JURASSIC 208-157 MYA	LATE JURASSIC 157-146 MYA

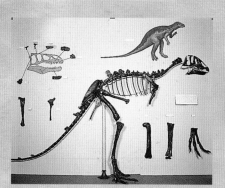

LIKE MEGALOSAURUS?

For a long time, the name *Megalosaurus* was applied to the fossil of any meat-eating dinosaur found in Britain or Europe. All kinds of unrelated dinosaurs were erroneously given the name. Only now is this mess of different animals being sorted out. There is a virtually complete skeleton of *Eustreptospondylus* in the Oxford University Museum in England. This was one of the dinosaurs once thought to be a *Megalosaurus*.

MEGALOSAURUS JAW

The lower jawbone and teeth of *Megalosaurus* were the first parts of the animal to be discovered. They were found in Oxfordshire, England, in about 1815. The Reverend William Buckland studied them and deduced from the sharp pointed teeth that they had belonged to a meat-eating animal, and that it had been a large reptile. Other scientists studied the remains in the 1820s and one of them—history does not tell us who—came up with the name *Megalosaurus*.

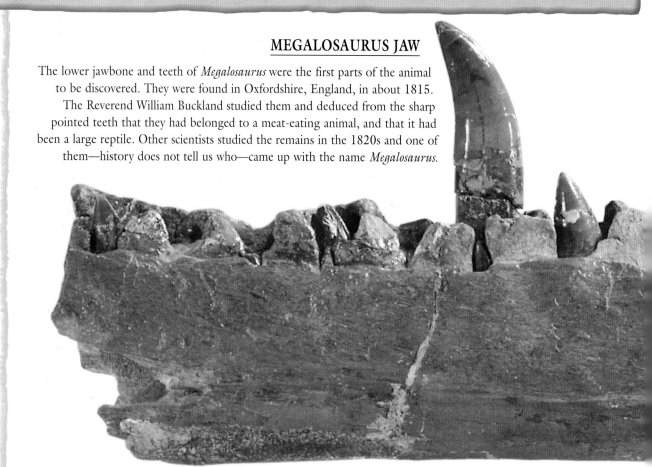

FIRST DINOSAUR THEME PARK

Because of the great public interest in science in the mid-19th century, part of Crystal Palace park in south London was developed as an ancient landscape. Statues (which still stand today) were erected showing the three dinosaurs and the marine reptiles that were known at the time. All that was known of *Megalosaurus* was its jawbone, teeth and a few fragments of bone. Since nobody knew what the animal actually looked like, it was modeled as a fearsome four-footed dragon-like creature.

TRIASSIC 245-208 MYA	EARLY/MID JURASSIC 208-157 MYA	LATE JURASSIC 157-146 MYA	EARLY CRETACEOUS 146-97 MYA	LATE CRETACEOUS 97-65 MYA

THE FIRST KNOWN

Since civilization began, people have known about giant bones embedded in the rocks. In earlier times they were spoken of in legends as the bones of giants and dragons and other mythical creatures. By the early 19th century, however, scientific knowledge had advanced sufficiently for scientists to begin to appreciate the true nature of fossils. In 1842, the British anatomist, Sir Richard Owen, invented the term "dinosauria" (terrible lizards) to classify three fossil animals whose skeletons had been discovered in England during the previous two decades. One was the plant-eating *Iguanodon*, which is now quite well known. Another was the armored *Hylaeosaurus*, which we still know very little about. The first of the trio to be brought to light and described was the carnivorous *Megalosaurus*.

WILLIAM BUCKLAND (1784–1856)

This 19th-century clergyman was typical of his time. When not in the pulpit he spent his extensive spare time doing scientific research. Most of the fossils he studied were those of sea-living animals—seashells and marine reptiles. Fossils of land-living animals have always been rarer. He may not have invented the name *Megalosaurus* but he was the scholar who did all the scientific work on it.

MODERN VIEW

Even today, we do not have a clear idea of what *Megalosaurus* looked like because so few fossilized remains have been found. Like all meat-eating dinosaurs, it must have walked on its hind legs with its big head held well forward, balanced by a heavy tail. Fossils found in lagoon deposits in what is now Normandy in northern France suggest that *Megalosaurus* was a shoreline scavenger that prowled along the beach, eating the dead things that had been washed up.

EARLY HUNTERS

Most of the early meat-eating dinosaurs were small animals, some no bigger than our domestic cats and dogs. They probably fed mainly on even smaller animals, such as lizards and the early mammals. However, most of the plant-eating reptiles of the time were quite large animals and would also have made good prey for the meat-eaters. Some of the early dinosaurs adopted a strategy of hunting in packs so that they could bring down and kill some of these big plant-eaters. Today, such team-work is still used in the wild by animals such as Canadian wolves, which hunt moose much bigger than themselves. Similarly, on the African plains, groups of hyenas attack wildebeest that are far bigger than they are.

THE CONNECTICUT FOOTPRINTS

At the beginning of the 19th century, long before anybody knew anything about dinosaurs, farmers in New England, USA, kept finding three-toed trackways in the Triassic sandstone at the foot of the Appalachian Mountains, shown above. At first, it was believed the footprints were made by giant birds that had existed in the area before Noah's flood as described in the Bible. We now know they were footprints of dinosaur packs, probably made by *Coelophysis* or something similar.

TRIASSIC	EARLY/MID JURASSIC	LATE JURASSIC	EARLY CRETACEOUS	LATE CRETACEOUS
245-208 MYA	208-157 MYA	157-146 MYA	146-97 MYA	97-65 MYA

BIRD & DINOSAUR FOOTPRINTS

Birds and dinosaurs are so closely related it is little wonder the footprints of one could be mistaken for those of the other. In a series of ridges of Jurassic and Cretaceous rocks in the flanks of the Rocky Mountains west of Denver, USA, there are fossilized footprints of both dinosaurs and birds. Bird footprints can be distinguished from dinosaur prints by the greater spread of their toes—about 90° as opposed to about 45°. There is also often a trace of the little fourth toe pointing backwards. In dinosaurs, this toe is usually well clear of the ground.

DINOSAUR

BIRD

ONE WORLD

In late Triassic and early Jurassic times the world was very different from the way it is today. All the continental landmasses were joined together in one area called Pangaea. Since there was only one landmass, animals of the same kind were able to migrate everywhere. This is why we find the remains of almost identical animals in New Mexico and Connecticut, USA, as well as in Zimbabwe, thousands of miles away on the African continent.

SYNTARSUS

In 1972, a remarkable deposit of fossils was found in Rhodesia (now Zimbabwe). A mass of bones lay in fine river sediment, sandwiched between rocks formed from sand dunes. The fossils were of a pack of small meat-eating dinosaurs of different sizes and ages. They seemed to have drowned in a flash flood that struck as they were crossing a dry river bed. These meat-eating dinosaurs, named *Syntarsus*, were almost identical in build to *Coelophysis* and some scientists think they were a different species of the same animal.

COELOPHYSIS

Late Triassic *Coelophysis* was a 10-feet (3-m) long carnivore. In the 1940s, a whole group of them was discovered fossilized in New Mexico, evidently having perished in a drought. Since they had both lived and died together, it was deduced that these animals moved about in packs or family groups. Another behavioral trait came to light when the skeleton of a youngster was found in the stomach area of one of the adults. Perhaps they had been so desperate for food that they ate their own kind.

CREST-HEADED BEASTS

Look at the bright colors of many birds—the long tail feathers of a peacock, the gaudy bill of a toucan, the red breast of a robin. Color is part of a bird's method of communication. Their brain can "read" the colors they see and enables them to recognize whether another bird is a friend or foe. Birds are related to dinosaurs, which had similar brains and senses. It is very likely that dinosaurs also used color for communication. Some dinosaurs (especially among the carnivores) had crests and horns as brightly colored as the plumage of modern birds.

DAZZLING DILOPHOSAURUS

In life, *Dilophosaurus* probably looked dazzling. It seems very likely that its crests were particularly colorful either to frighten rivals or attract a mate from far away. The rest of the animal may also have been brightly colored to back up the signals given by the crests. Dewlaps (flaps of skin beneath the chin) may have been brightly colored like modern lizards, and would also have been part of the display

FORWARD THINKING

The early Jurassic meat-eater from Antarctica, *Cryolophosaurus*, had a crest that curled up and forwards above its eyes. The bony core was probably covered in brightly-colored horn or skin. *Cryolophosaurus* is the only dinosaur known to have had a crest that ran across the skull rather than along it. At 26 feet (8 m) long, it was probably the biggest meat-eater of its time, its size enhanced still further by its crest.

HORNED MONSTER

In the late Jurassic, one of the fiercest of the dinosaurs was *Ceratosaurus*, 20 feet (6 m) long. It lived in North America and Tanzania in East Africa. *Ceratosaurus* had a heavy head with a horn on the nose and another pair of horns above the eyes. The heavy skull suggests they may have fought with one another by head-battering, but the horns were very lightly built and would not have been much use as weapons. They may have been used only for display, and perhaps only the males had them for courtship rituals.

MONOLOPHOSAURUS

The crest of *Monolophosaurus*, a medium-sized middle Jurassic meat-eating dinosaur from China, was made up of a pair of skull bones fused together and growing upwards. Air gaps and channels between these bones were connected to the nostrils and may have been used to amplify grunts and roars generated in the animal's throat. In this way the crest would have helped *Monolophosaurus* communicate by sound as well as visually.

DILOPHOSAURUS SKELETON

Dilophosaurus was a bear-sized, meat-eating dinosaur from the early Jurassic of North America. The first skeleton found had semicircular plate-like structures lying near it. Later finds showed that these structures were crests that ran parallel to one another along the length of the skull. However, what no skeleton can ever tell us is what color the crests were in life.

TRIASSIC	EARLY/MID JURASSIC	LATE JURASSIC	EARLY CRETACEOUS	LATE CRETACEOUS
245-208 MYA	208-157 MYA	157-146 MYA	146-97 MYA	97-65 MYA

HEAVY CLAW

Baryonyx was discovered by an amateur fossil collector in southern England in 1983. The skeleton was so complete that it gave us the first clear view of what these animals looked like. *Baryonyx* was an unusual meat-eating dinosaur that had crocodile-like jaws packed with sharp teeth, and long forelimbs with hooked claws, which were used to catch fish.

Baryonyx stood 10 feet (3 m) tall, and each of its claws measured nearly 12 inches (35 cm) long. It probably ranged over a large area stretching from England to North Africa.

SPINOSAURUS

MENACING MIMIC

Suchomimus fossils were found in a remote dune-covered area of the Sahara in 1998 by a team from the United States and Niger. An enormous predatory dinosaur with a skull like a crocodile's and huge thumb claws, it measured 36 feet (11 m) in length and 12 feet (4 m) high at the hip. The thumb claws and powerfully built forelimbs were used to snare prey, and the thin sail along its back, which reached a height of 2 feet (50 cm) over the hips, may have been brightly colored for display.

SPINOSAURUS—50 feet (15 m) long, 24 feet (7 m) high
SUCHOMIMUS—36 feet (11 m) long, 12 feet (4 m) high
BARYONYX—32 feet (10 m) long, 10 feet (3 m) high
IRRITATOR—21 feet (6 m) long, 6 feet (2 m) high

BARYONYX

BIG BITE

Many modern reptiles have similarities to the spinosaurids. Crocodiles and alligators, for example, have long jaws and many teeth, and hunt for fish in a similar way. Like the spinosaurids, scientists also wrongly suspected crocodiles and alligators of eating their own young.

SPINOSAURIDS: THE FISH EATERS

We normally think of fish-eating animals as creatures that live in the water. However, there are many land-living animals that like to eat fish too. Grizzly bears are often seen beside waterfalls hooking out migrating salmon as they leap up to their spawning grounds, and otters live mostly on land but hunt fish. It was the same in the Jurassic period. One particular family of land-dwelling dinosaurs—the spinosaurids—seem to have been particularly well-equipped for fishing. They had long jaws with many small teeth, and a big claw on each hand. They lived in early Cretaceous times, and their remains have been found across the world, from Southern England to North Africa and South America.

SUCHOMIMUS

IRRITATOR

SPINY CUSTOMER

Spinosaurus was excavated in Egypt in 1912. Unfortunately, its remains were destroyed when the museum where they were stored in Germany was bombed in World War II. What we do know about it was that it was as big as *Tyrannosaurus* and had a fin down its back, almost 6½ feet (2 m) tall. The fin was probably used to cool the animal in hot weather. In 1999, an American expedition found its original quarry in Egypt, so there may be hope of finding new specimens in the future.

HERE'S ONE I MADE EARLIER

Irritator was given its name because of the confusing circumstances in which it was found. The skull—all that we have of the animal—was collected in Brazil sometime in the 1990s and sent to a museum in Stuttgart, Germany. But then the museum staff had a surprise. Whoever dug it up and sold it to the museum had added pieces to it and stuck it together with car body filler to make it look much more spectacular. Now that we have had a proper look at it, we can tell that it is a small spinosaurid.

TRIASSIC 245-208 MYA	EARLY/MID JURASSIC 208-157 MYA	LATE JURASSIC 157-146 MYA	EARLY CRETACEOUS 146-97 MYA	LATE CRETACEOUS 97-65 MYA

NQWEBASAURUS

Scientists became very excited in the late 1990s when they found the almost complete skeleton of 3-feet (1-m) long *Nqwebasaurus* embedded in early Cretaceous rocks in South Africa. It proved that the family to which most of the small meat-eating dinosaurs belonged (the coelurosaurids) had existed in the southern continents during the Cretaceous period, as well as in North America, Europe, and Asia.

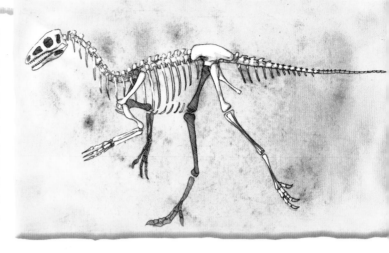

ITALIAN BEAUTY

In the 1990s, this beautifully-preserved skeleton of *Scipionyx* was found in early Cretaceous rocks in Italy. It was so finely fossilized that even some of the soft anatomy (the lungs and guts) were preserved. Their existence confirms that this animal, probably along with all other small dinosaurs, was able to breathe efficiently while running. This would have made it an energetic and active hunter. The way the bones were articulated indicate that this specimen of *Scipionyx*, only 10 inches (25 cm) long, was not yet fully grown.

TINIEST FOOTPRINT

In the 1970s, the tiny footprint of a dinosaur that could have been no bigger than a thrush was found in the late Triassic rocks of Newfoundland in Canada. The arrangement of the toes is typical of the meat-eating dinosaurs of the Triassic. The print is the only trace we have of the smallest dinosaur ever found. Whether it was a youngster or fully grown, nobody yet knows.

THE SMALLEST DINOSAURS

When we think about dinosaurs (terrible lizards), we usually visualize huge and fierce animals—they are the ones that have captured our imagination. However, some dinosaurs were actually small beasts not much bigger than a chicken. Scuttling about the ground among the giants, small dinosaurs were probably more common than the big ones. Unfortunately, as their bones were so lightweight and their skeletons quite delicate, very few have been preserved as fossils. Nevertheless, a number of good specimens have been found and some of these were preserved in great detail.

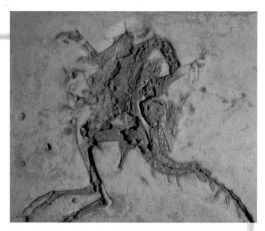

COMPSOGNATHUS SKELETON

Two *Compsognathus* skeletons have been found: one in France, the other in Germany. The German specimen was particularly well-preserved in fine limestone. Not only can we see the skeleton but also the contents of its stomach, showing that its last meal included a small lizard. Some scientists thought *Compsognathus* was the baby of some other type of dinosaur but the blobs scattered around the skeleton are probably eggs, as yet unlaid when the animal died. They suggest this *Compsognathus* was an adult female.

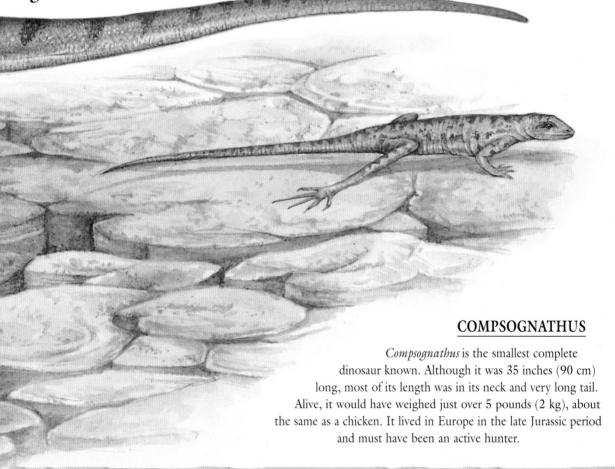

COMPSOGNATHUS

Compsognathus is the smallest complete dinosaur known. Although it was 35 inches (90 cm) long, most of its length was in its neck and very long tail. Alive, it would have weighed just over 5 pounds (2 kg), about the same as a chicken. It lived in Europe in the late Jurassic period and must have been an active hunter.

TRIASSIC 245-208 MYA	EARLY/MID JURASSIC 208-157 MYA	LATE JURASSIC 157-146 MYA	EARLY CRETACEOUS 146-97 MYA	LATE CRETACEOUS 97-65 MYA

JURASSIC GIANT

SKULL

A typical *Allosaurus* skull is about 3½ feet (1 m) long. The jaws were armed with more than 70 teeth, some measuring 3 inches (8 cm). The teeth were curved, pointed and serrated, ideal for ripping the flesh of large plant-eating dinosaurs. The joints between the skull bones would have allowed the snout to move up and down to help manipulate food. The lower jaws were hinged so they could expand sideways to allow the animal to gulp down big chunks of meat.

Some dinosaurs really did live up to their reputation of being enormous fearsome beasts. Probably the most terrifying animal of the late Jurassic period was *Allosaurus*. Its remains have been found in both Tanzania, Africa, and in the sequence of rocks known as the Morrison Formation which stretches down the western United States from the Canadian border to New Mexico. These deposits yielded the most important dinosaur discoveries made in the second half of the 19th century. Over a hundred different kinds of dinosaur (mostly plant-eaters) were found there. The most powerful of the meat-eaters found was *Allosaurus*.

MUSCLES

By studying the arrangement of bones in the skeleton and seeing the points of attachment for individual muscles, scientists have worked out what the fleshed-up *Allosaurus* would have looked like. The leg muscles would have allowed it to move at speeds of up to 18 mph (30 km/h)—not particularly swift but fast enough to catch the slow-moving herbivores of the time. The neck muscles would have been massive to control the huge head and powerful jaws.

FEET

The feet of *Allosaurus* had three powerful toes, muscular enough to carry the entire weight of the adult, which must have been over a ton (tonne). Unlike its fingers, the toes were not equipped with hooked claws but with broad hooves that would have helped to bear the great weight. The legs were not particularly long for the size of animal and were evidently not built for speed.

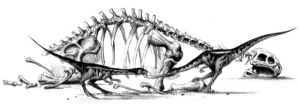

HUNTING

The bones of plant-eaters such as *Camarasaurus* are found throughout the Morrison Formation, often mixed up with the broken teeth of meat-eating dinosaurs. Discoveries like these suggest that the big plant-eaters—especially sick ones—were often attacked and killed by big meat-eaters like *Allosaurus*. Once the killer had eaten its fill, packs of smaller meat-eaters, such as *Ceratosaurus*, may have scavenged what was left. Anything left over would have been eaten by smaller animals.

FOREARMS

Allosaurus' hands had three claws: one claw, at 10 inches (25 cm) long, was much larger than the other two. The joint on this first finger allowed the huge claw to turn inwards. *Allosaurus* would have been able to grasp its prey, kill it, then rip it apart. The span of its hand would have been wide enough to grasp the head of an adult man, if humans had existed in Jurassic times!

ALLOSAURUS IN LIFE

We have a fairly good idea what *Allosaurus* looked like from the thousands of bone specimens (some almost complete skeletons) that have been found. These bones belonged to juveniles that measured about 10 feet (3 m) from nose to tail-tip, and to adults of about 30 feet (9 m) long. Some of the *Allosaurus* bones found must have come from 40-feet (12-m) monsters. Mounted casts of *Allosaurus* skeletons can be seen in many museums around the world, including the Field Museum in Chicago. The actual bones are usually kept behind the scenes for research.

TRIASSIC 245-208 MYA	EARLY/MID JURASSIC 208-157 MYA	LATE JURASSIC 157-146 MYA	EARLY CRETACEOUS 146-97 MYA	LATE CRETACEOUS 97-65 MYA

FAST HUNTERS

Back in the late 19th/early 20th century there was a theory that birds and dinosaurs were related. This theory fell out of favor for a long time but was revived in the 1960s when a group of dinosaurs, extremely bird-like in their build, were discovered. They ranged from the size of a goose to the size of a tiger and had wing-like joints in their forearms. They also had strong hind legs with huge, sickle-like killing claws on their feet, showing that they were very fast runners and fierce hunters. These dinosaurs are known as the dromaeosaurids (part of a larger group called the maniraptorans) and are commonly referred to as the "raptors."

BIRD OR DROMAEOSAURID?

Right down to the killing claw on its foot *Rahonavis*, an early Cretaceous bird from Madagascar, had the skeleton of a dromaeosaurid. If it had not been for the functional wings, many scientists would have grouped it with the dromaeosaurids.

TERRIBLE CLAWS

The skeleton of a plant-eating *Tenontosaurus*, found in late Cretaceous rocks in Montana, USA, was surrounded by the remains of several *Deinonychus*. This suggests that *Deinonychus* hunted in packs, surrounded a prey animal and then slashed it to death. With its big brain and balancing tail, a *Deinonychus* could have stood on one foot and slashed its prey with the other, or it may have hung on to its victim with its clawed hands and slashed away with both hind feet, as cats do. Judging from the remains the *Tenontosaurus* must have put up a fight and killed some of its attackers before it died.

UTAHRAPTOR

DEINONYCHUS

VELOCIRAPTOR

BAMBIRAPTOR

A RANGE OF DROMAEOSAURIDS

About the size of a goose, *Bambiraptor* is the smallest of the dromaeosaurids. Turkey-sized *Velociraptor* is probably the best-known. Scientists were first alerted to the bird-like nature of these animals in the 1960s, when tiger-sized *Deinonychus* was discovered. Bigger dromaeosaurids are known but only from bone fragments. *Utahraptor* probably weighed more than a ton (tonne) while *Megaraptor* (not shown), known only from a 13-inch (34-cm) killing claw, must have approached the size of the big meat-eaters, such as *Allosaurus*. Apart from the Argentinian *Megaraptor*, all these animals were found in late Cretaceous rocks in North America.

EARLY BIRD

This fossil of the first bird Archaeopteryx, dating from the late Jurassic period, was found in Germany in 1877. If it had not been for the feather impressions in the fossil, the skeleton would have been mistaken for that of a dinosaur because it has a toothed jaw, clawed hands, and a long tail. As well as developing into modern birds, it is possible that some of *Archaeopteryx's* descendants lost their powers of flight and developed into the dromaeosaurids and other related meat-eating dinosaurs of the Cretaceous period. They were certainly closely related to one another.

BAMBIRAPTOR

Any doubts about whether or not dromaeosaurids were related to birds were finally put to rest in the late 1990s, when an almost complete skeleton of *Bambiraptor* was discovered in late Cretaceous rocks in Montana, USA. Every bone seems to be a bird bone, every joint a bird joint. It was no doubt a warm-blooded animal, covered with feathers.

TRIASSIC 245-208 MYA	EARLY/MID JURASSIC 208-157 MYA	LATE JURASSIC 157-146 MYA	EARLY CRETACEOUS 146-97 MYA	LATE CRETACEOUS 97-65 MYA

TROODON

Troodon was one of the maniraptorans, although it was not quite as bird-like as the dromaeosaurids. This small meat-eater of the late Cretaceous period was about 8 feet (2.5 m) long and may well have had feathers.

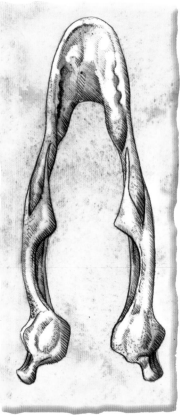

CAENAGNATHUS JAWBONE

Caenagnathus was a dinosaur that probably resembled *Oviraptor*, and may have been an egg eater. Certainly, its toothless lower jaw was quite wide in the middle and would have been good for swallowing eggs. As no other remains have ever been found, *Caenagnathus* remains a bit of a mystery.

OVIRAPTOR HEAD

An *Oviraptor's* head makes it easy to believe it might be an egg eater. Its very short, beak-like mouth and its gullet, situated right over the widest part of its jaw, were ideal for swallowing something big and round. As in modern egg-eating snakes, two bones protruding down from its palate were perfectly positioned to tear open an egg on its way down. With its long fingers, just right for grasping eggs, *Oviraptor* may after all have been an egg-eating dinosaur. There seems to have been little else for it to eat on the desert plains of late Cretaceous Mongolia.

EGG THIEF

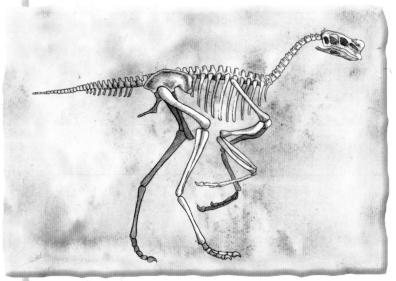

The jaw of *Caenagnathus* was similar to that of *Chirostenotes*. This was a turkey-sized dinosaur with very long fingers that would have enabled it to raid other dinosaur nests for their eggs. Perhaps there were many different kinds of egg-stealing dinosaurs in late Cretaceous times.

TRIASSIC 245-208 MYA	EARLY/MID JURASSIC 208-157 MYA	LATE JURASSIC 157-146 MYA	EARLY CRETACEOUS 146-97 MYA	LATE CRETACEOUS 97-65 MYA

EGGS & NESTS

Like modern birds, some dinosaurs built nests and laid eggs. The first known dinosaur nests were found by an expedition sent to the Gobi desert by the American Museum of Natural History in 1923. The nests were among remains of herds of the horned dinosaur *Protoceratops*. Alongside the supposed *Protoceratops* eggs lay the skeleton of a toothless meat-eater *Oviraptor*. This so-called "egg thief" was thought to have been buried in a sandstorm while digging up the eggs. But, as sometimes happens, more evidence caused later palaeontologists to re-evaluate this interpretation. In the 1990s, another expedition to the Gobi desert found the fossil of an *Oviraptor* sitting on a nest, incubating eggs, which suggested those first nests were also *Oviraptor* nests!

TROODON EGGS

Fossils of *Troodon* nests show they were oval ridges of mud surrounding the eggs, very much like the nests of *Oviraptor*. The eggs were laid in pairs which suggests that the dinosaur had a pair of oviducts (egg tubes) within its body. A modern bird has only one oviduct. Birds have developed many such features which keep down their body weight to make flying easier.

NESTING DINOSAUR

In the 1990s, a fossil was found of an *Oviraptor* sitting on a nest with its arms spread protectively around some eggs, evidently keeping them warm with the heat of its body. Modern birds do this efficiently as their feathers provide excellent insulation. This is one of the indirect lines of evidence that suggests that *Oviraptor*, and many other bird-like dinosaurs, had feathers.

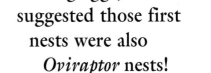

BIRD OR DINOSAUR?

As well as finding the first dinosaur nests, the American expeditions to the Gobi desert in the 1920s uncovered many other dinosaur remains. One of these we now call *Mononykus* is a total puzzle. Was it a bird or was it a dinosaur? If it was a bird, its arms were too short for it to fly. If it was a dinosaur, what good were hands reduced to a single finger with a big claw? In the 1980s, when new specimens were found, *Mononykus* was found to have belonged to a group of related animals, the alvarezsaurids—a distinct group within the maniraptorans—that ranged from South America to Central Asia. Sadly, we still do not know whether they were birds or dinosaurs even today.

MONONYKUS

The best known and most complete of the alvarezsaurids was *Mononykus*. It looked like a very lightly-built, meat-eating dinosaur with spindly legs and a long tail. The two forelimbs are remarkable. They are short and have a shelf of bone, which in modern birds would support wing feathers, and each bears a single stout stubby claw. These forelimbs probably developed from the functional wings of a flying ancestor, such as the late Jurassic *Archaeopteryx*.

OSTRICH

One function of non-flying wings in modern running birds is for display. The ostrich makes a big show of its wing feathers when it is courting a mate or threatening an enemy. It is quite possible that the part-bird/part-dinosaur animals of the Cretaceous period also had flamboyant feathers on their flightless wings and used them for display. Unfortunately, such behavior cannot be proven by fossil evidence.

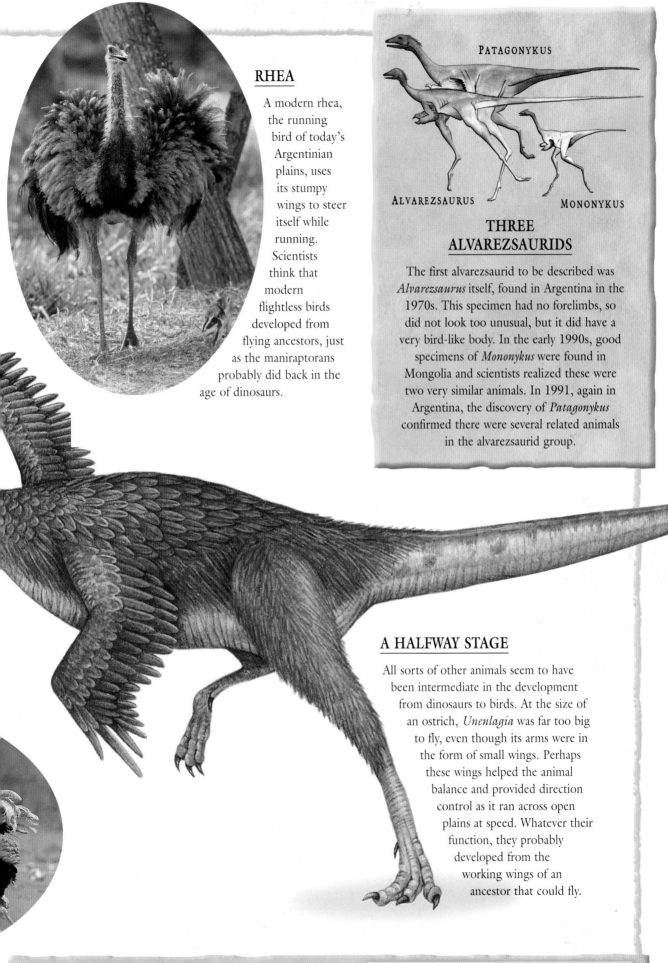

RHEA

A modern rhea, the running bird of today's Argentinian plains, uses its stumpy wings to steer itself while running. Scientists think that modern flightless birds developed from flying ancestors, just as the maniraptorans probably did back in the age of dinosaurs.

PATAGONYKUS

ALVAREZSAURUS

MONONYKUS

THREE ALVAREZSAURIDS

The first alvarezsaurid to be described was *Alvarezsaurus* itself, found in Argentina in the 1970s. This specimen had no forelimbs, so did not look too unusual, but it did have a very bird-like body. In the early 1990s, good specimens of *Mononykus* were found in Mongolia and scientists realized these were two very similar animals. In 1991, again in Argentina, the discovery of *Patagonykus* confirmed there were several related animals in the alvarezsaurid group.

A HALFWAY STAGE

All sorts of other animals seem to have been intermediate in the development from dinosaurs to birds. At the size of an ostrich, *Unenlagia* was far too big to fly, even though its arms were in the form of small wings. Perhaps these wings helped the animal balance and provided direction control as it ran across open plains at speed. Whatever their function, they probably developed from the working wings of an ancestor that could fly.

| TRIASSIC 245-208 MYA | EARLY/MID JURASSIC 208-157 MYA | LATE JURASSIC 157-146 MYA | EARLY CRETACEOUS 146-97 MYA | LATE CRETACEOUS 97-65 MYA |

TERRIBLE HAND

An intriguing fossil from late Cretaceous rocks in Mongolia shows a pair of arms, 8 feet (2.5 m) long, with three-clawed hands. The animal has been given the name *Deinocheirus* but we know nothing else about it. The bones look as if they are from an ornithomimid but they are far bigger than those of any known member of this group. For now, the owner of these extraordinary bones remains a mystery.

GALLIMIMUS SKELETON

Gallimimus is probably the best known of the Ornithomimids. It had a small toothless beak, which it used for cropping fruit and vegetation. This dinosaur was built for speed, and could run at up to 50 mph (80 km/h), as fast as a racehorse. It usually paced around slowly, stalking small mammals or snapping up seeds and insects, but its speed meant that it could escape from most predators. Its long tail acted as a counterbalance to the front of the body, propelling it forward while it sprinted. Its hipbone also pointed forward. This skeleton is mounted on display at the Natural History Museum in London, England.

STRUTHIOMIMUS

ORNITHOMIMIDS

All ornithomimids looked similar but varied somewhat in size. *Struthiomimus* was about the size of an ostrich. *Pelecanimimus* was smaller and many scientists think it was one of the earliest in the group to develop. It had a pouch of skin beneath its long jaws, which had hundreds of tiny teeth in them. This suggests the teeth of the group became smaller and smaller before disappearing altogether in the later ornithomimids. *Garidumimus*, named after a mythical Hindu bird, had a small crest on its head. The biggest known was *Gallimimus*, the "chicken mimic," at 13–16 feet (4–5 m) long. Some chicken!

TRIASSIC 245-208 MYA	EARLY/MID JURASSIC 208-157 MYA	LATE JURASSIC 157-146 MYA	EARLY CRETACEOUS 146-97 MYA	LATE CRETACEOUS 97-65 MYA

BIRD MIMICS

One group of dinosaurs has always been thought to look very much like birds. Ornithomimids (bird mimics) had plump, compact bodies; big eyes; toothless beaks on small heads that were supported on long, slender necks, and long running legs with thick muscles close to the hip. Typical of the group was a dinosaur called *Struthiomimus* (ostrich mimic) from the late Cretaceous period. Although they fall into the category of meat-eating dinosaurs and would have descended from purely carnivorous ancestors, these dinosaurs were probably omnivorous, eating fruit and leaves as well as insects and small vertebrates, such as lizards. Ostriches and other ground birds of today are also omnivores.

BUILT FOR SPEED

As with most meat-eating dinosaurs the skeleton of an ornithomimid, such as this *ornithomimus*, is very bird-like. Its head would have been held farther forward than that of an ostrich, balanced by its long tail. However, they had very similar legs with a very short femur (thighbone) that would have held all the muscles so that the lower leg and the toes were worked only by tendons. This gives a very lightweight leg that could move quickly—a running leg.

GALLIMIMUS

GARIDUMIMUS

PELECANIMIMUS

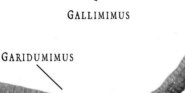

EMU

A modern emu is a typical plains-living animal. The keen eyes in the head, held high on the top of a long neck, are able to spot danger coming from a long way away across the open spaces. The strong running legs are then able to take the bird out of danger at great speed. Because of the physical similarity, many scientists think that the ornithomimids of the late Cretaceous period had a similar lifestyle on the plains of North America and central Asia.

ERLIKOSAURUS SKULL

The best known segnosaurid skull is that of *Erlikosaurus*. It looks very much like the skulls of some of the big plant-eating dinosaurs. Behind its toothless beak the teeth are small and leaf-shaped. Some scientists have suggested this might be the skull of a fish-eating dinosaur and that the foot bones (which are also unusual) could have been webbed for swimming. However, the rest of the skeleton suggests that it could not have been a swimming animal.

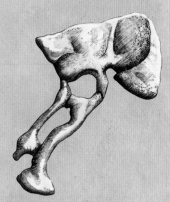

SEGNOSAURUS HIPBONE

The hipbones of meat-eating dinosaurs are usually quite distinctive. The pubis bone at the front points forwards. In the segnosaurids, the pubis bone sweeps backwards. This is usually only seen in plant-eating dinosaurs, as it gives more space for the big plant-eating gut that such animals need. It would have given the body of this dinosaur a very dumpy appearance. This is part of what makes the whole group a puzzle.

SEGNOSAURIDS

Sometimes, fossils are so unlike any known dinosaur that nobody knows what kind of creature they are. Such is the case with the segnosaurids. In the 1920s, the first fossils, found in late Cretaceous rocks in Mongolia, were thought to be from a giant turtle, but were re-classified as dinosaur remains in the 1970s. The various bits of bone were all so unalike they seemed to be from different families of dinosaur. Even now, the name therizinosaurid is sometimes used for the group; the name was first used as the original classification of the forelimb, as opposed to segnosaurid, the name set up when the skull and backbone were studied. These dinosaurs were thought to be meat-eaters; then to be prosauropods, one of the long-necked plant-eaters. These days most scientists classify them with the meat-eaters.

A MODERN PARALLEL

The anteater is a modern animal with claws that seem too big for its body. It uses them to rip through the tough walls of anthills to get at the living chambers of the ant colony. Some scientists have suggested that this is how the segnosaurids lived, while others doubt this diet could have supported such a big animal.

TRIASSIC 245-208 MYA	EARLY/MID JURASSIC 208-157 MYA	LATE JURASSIC 157-146 MYA	EARLY CRETACEOUS 146-97 MYA	LATE CRETACEOUS 97-65 MYA

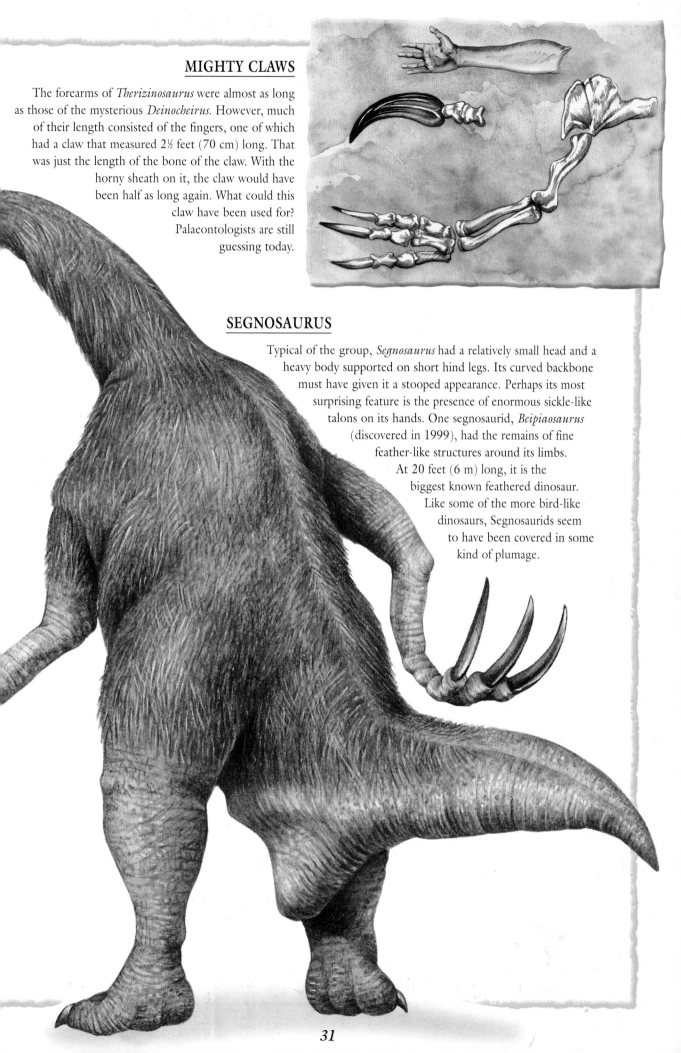

MIGHTY CLAWS

The forearms of *Therizinosaurus* were almost as long as those of the mysterious *Deinocheirus*. However, much of their length consisted of the fingers, one of which had a claw that measured 2½ feet (70 cm) long. That was just the length of the bone of the claw. With the horny sheath on it, the claw would have been half as long again. What could this claw have been used for? Palaeontologists are still guessing today.

SEGNOSAURUS

Typical of the group, *Segnosaurus* had a relatively small head and a heavy body supported on short hind legs. Its curved backbone must have given it a stooped appearance. Perhaps its most surprising feature is the presence of enormous sickle-like talons on its hands. One segnosaurid, *Beipiaosaurus* (discovered in 1999), had the remains of fine feather-like structures around its limbs. At 20 feet (6 m) long, it is the biggest known feathered dinosaur. Like some of the more bird-like dinosaurs, Segnosaurids seem to have been covered in some kind of plumage.

TYRANNOSAURIDS

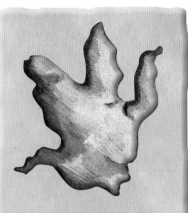

FOOTPRINT

In the late 1980s, a dinosaur footprint almost 3 feet (1 m) long was discovered on a slab of late Cretaceous rock in New Mexico. Whatever beast made it had a meat-eater's claws. There was only one print, so the stride of the animal must have been greater than the almost 10-feet (3-m) long slab of rock. Scientists estimate the animal was moving at 5–6 mph (8–10 km/h). We cannot be sure this footprint was made by a *Tyrannosaurus*, but we know of no bigger meat-eating dinosaurs in Cretaceous North America.

At 39 feet (12 m) long and 20 feet (6 m) tall, *Tyrannosaurus* must have been the scourge of the North American continent at the end of the dinosaur age. So far, about 15 specimens of *Tyrannosaurus* have been discovered in various states of completeness. From these we have built up a picture of what the mighty beasts looked like. However, there is still much debate about how they lived. Some scientists think they actively hunted, perhaps waiting to ambush duckbilled dinosaurs, the big plant-eaters of the time, charging out at them from the cover of the forest. Others insist they were too big for such activity but would have scavenged carrion, the meat of already-dead animals. Maybe they did both.

A RANGE OF TYRANNOSAURIDS

Daspletosaurus from North America was similar to *Tyrannosaurus* but was a little smaller and had a heavy head with fewer but larger teeth. At about 20 feet (6 m) long, *Alioramus* was a medium-sized tyrannosaurid from Asia. It had along skull with knobbles and spikes along the top. Some scientists think that the smallest was *Nanotyrannus*, from Montana, USA, which was about 13 feet (4 m) long, although other experts suspect that *Nanotyrannus* may actually be a small *Albertosaurus*, the one skull available to study was certainly from an adult animal.

NANOTYRANNUS

FRIGHTFUL BITE

Tyrannosaurus had incredibly powerful jaws and teeth used to rip flesh from its prey. Gouges in the pelvic bone of a late Cretaceous specimen of the three-horned dinosaur *Triceratops* exactly match the size and spacing of the teeth of *Tyrannosaurus*. From these marks scientists could tell that a *Tyrannosaurus* bit down into the meat of the hind leg and tore it away from the bone when the *Triceratops* was already dead. But whether or not it was the *Tyrannosaurus* that killed it, nobody can tell.

TYRANT LIZARD KING

Tyrannosaurus, the biggest of the tyrannosaurids, is often known by its full species name *Tyrannosaurus rex* or simply *T. rex*. Other dinosaurs also have full species names, such as *Allosaurus atrox*, *Velociraptor mongoliensis* and so on, but these are usually only used by scientists.

DASPLETOSAURUS

ALIORAMUS

COPROLITE

Fossilized animal droppings are known to geologists as coprolites and they give useful clues to an extinct animal's diet. But, as with footprints, it is often impossible to tell what animal made which coprolite. Big coprolites, more than 8 inches (20 cm) long, that may have come from *Tyrannosaurus*, have been found to contain smashed-up undigested bone fragments.

TRIASSIC	EARLY/MID JURASSIC	LATE JURASSIC	EARLY CRETACEOUS	LATE CRETACEOUS
245-208 MYA	208-157 MYA	157-146 MYA	146-97 MYA	97-65 MYA

MONSTROUS SKULL

The skull of *Carcharodontosaurus* is almost completely known.
When putting the skull bones together the scientists only had to
recreate the missing front of the snout and the bones at the very rear.
This they could do by drawing on their knowledge of other skulls.
The final skull is 5 feet (1.5 m) long and had strong, curved, shark-
like teeth. We know far less about the skull of *Giganotosaurus*. What we can be
sure of is that the jaws were not as powerful as those of *Tyrannosaurus*, the
teeth were not as strong and it had an even smaller
brain than the Tyrant Lizard King.

CARCHARODONTOSAURUS

Related to the Jurassic *Allosaurus*, *Carcharodontosaurus* came from Morocco,
Africa. Some fossils of it were first discovered by a German expedition in the
early 20th century but they were destroyed when their museum was bombed
during World War II, along with the original remains of *Spinosaurus* found on
the same expedition. Only when more fossils were discovered in the
mid–1990s did palaeontologists realize that *Carcharodontosaurus*
was a giant 50 feet (15 m) long.

TRIASSIC 245-208 MYA	EARLY/MID JURASSIC 208-157 MYA	LATE JURASSIC 157-146 MYA	EARLY CRETACEOUS 146-97 MYA	LATE CRETACEOUS 97-65 MYA

THE NEW KINGS

What was the biggest, strongest and fiercest meat-eating dinosaur that ever lived? *Tyrannosaurus?* Not any more! For the past hundred years we have said that *Tyrannosaurus* was the most powerful of the meat-eating dinosaurs. Generations of scientists have believed this to be so and have even stated that it would be mechanically impossible for bigger meat-eating animals to have existed. But the remains of even bigger meat-eaters have been found. In the 1990s, the skeletons of two carnivorous dinosaurs were found within a year of one another: one in South America, the other in Africa. Although neither skeleton was complete, they appear to have belonged to a group of dinosaurs that were even longer than *Tyrannosaurus.*

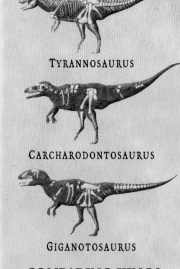

TYRANNOSAURUS

CARCHARODONTOSAURUS

GIGANOTOSAURUS

COMPARING KINGS

Both *Carcharodontosaurus* and *Giganotosaurus* were longer than the previous record-holder *Tyrannosaurus.* However, as shown above only *Tyrannosaurus* is known from complete skeletons and there is still a lot we don't know about the other two. Even so, *Tyrannosaurus* seems to have been a much heavier animal and was higher at the hip, so we could still say that the biggest meat-eating dinosaur that is completely known is still *Tyrannosaurus.*

GIGANOTOSAURUS

The great meat-eating dinosaur *Giganotosaurus* seems to have been closely related to *Carcharodontosaurus,* even though it lived in isolated South America in the late Cretaceous period while the other lived in Africa. It is likely that in the early part of the Cretaceous period, before the continents were separated by oceans, the ancestors of these animals spread across the whole world. After the continents split apart, *Giganotosaurus* began to develop separately.

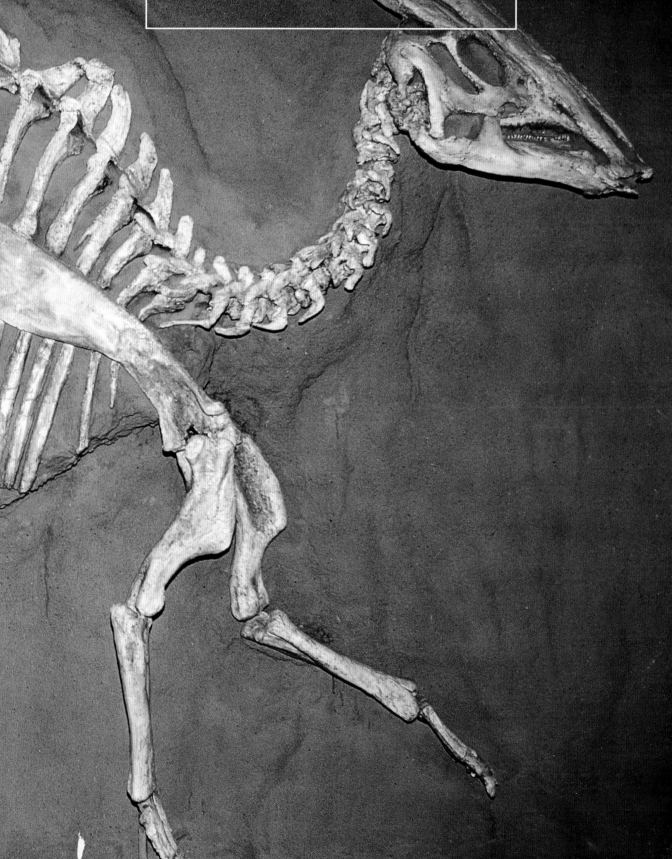

HERBIVORES

MUSSAURUS

The smallest dinosaur skeleton known belongs to a prosauropod. *Mussaurus* is small enough to be held in the the palm of a human hand. But we know it is the skeleton of a baby because the eyes and feet are bigger in relation to its body size than they would be in an adult, and its bones are not totally fused together.

An adult *Mussaurus* would have been about 10 feet (3 m) long.

SKULL COMPARISION BETWEEN A HERBIVORE AND CARNIVORE

PLATEOSAURUS

Jaw articulates below level of teeth.

Leaf-shaped teeth with continuous cutting edge.

Coarsly-serrated teeth for shredding leaves and shoots.

Teeth more or less the same size.

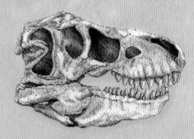

TYRANNOSAURUS

Jaw articulates at point level with teeth.

Strong, spike-shaped piercing teeth used for gripping and killing.

Finely-serrated saw-edged teeth like steak knives.

Teeth often break off and new ones grow in their place, creating a snaggle-toothed appearance.

DINOSAURS

RHYNCHOSAURS

MAMMAL-LIKE REPTILES

DEVELOPING VEGETATION

In the early part of the Reptile Age the most prolific plants were a kind of a fern that had seeds. They were the primary food source of the main plant-eating animals, the mammal-like reptiles. The seed ferns died away during the Triassic period, and ferns more like our modern species became common. Another group of reptiles, the rhynchosaurs, developed to eat them. At the end of the Triassic period, conifer trees spread everywhere and prosauropod dinosaurs developed to eat them.

THE FIRST PLANT-EATING DINOSAURS

Plant-eating dinosaurs (herbivores) were the real giants of the Age of the Dinosaurs. They included the mighty *Diplodocus* and *Seisomosaurus*, the largest animals ever to walk the Earth. Herbivorous reptiles are known from the early part of the Age of Reptiles, 350 million years ago. The first herbivorous dinosaurs developed in the late Triassic period, appearing about the same time as the carnivores. Because the hipbones in both groups of dinosaurs are similarly formed, we know that the plant-eaters must have developed from meat-eating dinosaurs.

PANGAEA

The world was very different in late Triassic/ early Jurassic times. The joining of land masses into the area called Pangaea meant that animals of the same kind could migrate everywhere. This is why we find the remains of almost identical animals all over the world, from Australia to America.

PLATEOSAURUS

The first plant-eating dinosaurs belonged to the prosauropod group. *Plateosaurus* was a typical prosauropod. It had a long neck and small head, but perhaps its most important feature was its big body. To process plant matter a herbivore needs a far greater volume of digestive gut than a carnivore. The prosauropod's heavy mass of intestines, carried well forward of the hips, would have made the animal too unbalanced to spend much time on its hind legs, so prosauropods became four-footers early in their history.

TRIASSIC	EARLY/MID JURASSIC	LATE JURASSIC	EARLY CRETACEOUS	LATE CRETACEOUS
245-208 MYA	208-157 MYA	157-146 MYA	146-97 MYA	97-65 MYA

HELPLESS PREY

Palaeontologists have found the remains of a prosauropod *Euskelosaurus* in late Triassic rocks in South Africa and Switzerland. The bones of its feet and legs are preserved, but the rest of the skeleton is broken up and scattered. Teeth of crocodile-like reptiles and carnivorous dinosaurs are among them. From this we suppose that *Euskelosaurus* became stuck in mud and, while struggling helplessly, was attacked by meat-eaters.

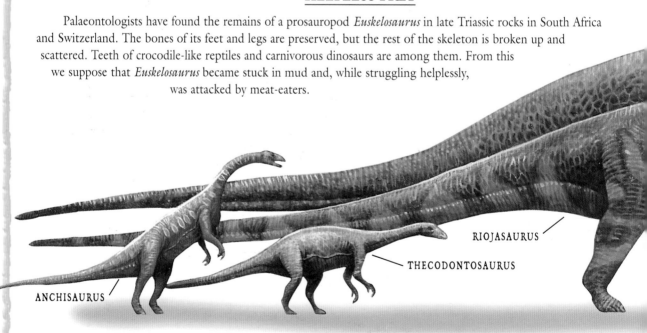

RIOJASAURUS

THECODONTOSAURUS

ANCHISAURUS

LIFE OF THE PROSAUROPODS

Ever since plants have existed plant-eating animals have fed on them, and ever since plant-eating animals have existed meat-eaters have, in turn, fed on them. This type of food chain can still be seen today on the grasslands of Africa where herds of herbivorous wildebeest and zebra graze on the low vegetation of the savannah and, in turn, are preyed upon by prowling carnivores such as lions and cheetahs. It was no different during the age of the dinosaurs. Prosauropods fed on the trees and were themselves stalked by the meat-eaters of the time, including the early carnivorous dinosaurs.

TRACKWAYS

The footprints called Navajopus from early Jurassic rocks of Arizona perfectly match the foot bones of a typical prosauropod, with the big hind feet and smaller front feet, each with four toes and inwardly-curved claws. They are likely to have been made by a small *Thecodontosaurus*-sized prosauropod called *Ammosaurus*.

MELANOROSAURUS

RANGE OF PROSAUROPODS

During the Triassic period, Sauropods ranged all over Pangaea, the world's landmass. *Melanorosaurus* lived in South Africa, *Thecodontosaurus* in western Europe, *Anchisaurus* in western North America, and *Riojasaurus* in South America. Other prosauropods, such as *Plateosaurus* and the Plateosaurus-like *Lufengosaurus* lived in what is now China. They were all extinct by middle Jurassic times.

TRIASSIC 245-208 MYA	EARLY/MID JURASSIC 208-157 MYA	LATE JURASSIC 157-146 MYA	EARLY CRETACEOUS 146-97 MYA	LATE CRETACEOUS 97-65 MYA

STOMACH STONES

The small head and mouth of sauropods were not designed for chewing. To help break down the food sauropods swallowed stones, which ground up plant material as it passed. We know this because gastroliths (stomach stones) have been found among their bones. Today, many plant-eating birds do the same.

SAUROPODS

The biggest of the dinosaurs were the long-necked plant-eaters known as sauropods (lizard feet). They had elephantine bodies, legs like tree trunks, relatively small heads on top of long necks, and long whip-like tails. They were related to the meat-eating dinosaurs and to the prosauropods, evolving in the early Jurassic, peaking in the late Jurassic and dying off in Cretaceous times.

DIPLODOCUS

Perhaps the best known of the long sauropods is *Diplodocus*. At 88 feet (27 m) long, it was one of several sauropods that roamed the plains and woodlands of North America in late Jurassic times. The way the neck bones were articulated tells us they browsed on low ferny vegetation, probably sweeping out great arcs with their long necks. The balance of muscles at the hips would also have enabled them to stretch up on their hind legs to reach the trees. The signs of wear on their teeth show they fed in both positions.

SAUROPOD FRAME

Remains of sauropod skeletons consist of massive pieces of fossilized bone, so big that there is nothing alive today with which scientists can compare them. In one of the latest techniques, very basic bone shapes are programmed into a computer and manipulated to let us see how the various pieces moved against one another. These studies are particularly useful for studying the flexibility of necks and tails.

TRACES OF LIFESTYLE

We used to think sauropods were too heavy to spend much time on land, and must have supported their vast bulk by wading in deep water. However, we now know (mostly from fossilized footprints) that sauropods moved about in herds on dry land. Large and small footprints found together show that different sauropods lived in groups. As there is no sign of tail marks in the tracks, they must have kept their tails raised.

SHUNOSAURUS

DIPLODOCUS

IN DEFENSE

Sauropods would have been prey to the big carnivorous dinosaurs. Just as today tigers do not attack fully-grown elephants, in Jurassic times the biggest of the sauropods would have been safe from the meat-eaters but the young and the sick would have been under constant threat. *Diplodocus* probably protected itself and its herd by using its long tapering tail as a whip. *Shunosaurus*, which lived in China during the middle Jurassic, probably used the small club on the end of its tail to defend itself.

| TRIASSIC 245-208 MYA | EARLY/MID JURASSIC 208-157 MYA | LATE JURASSIC 157-146 MYA | EARLY CRETACEOUS 146-97 MYA | LATE CRETACEOUS 97-65 MYA |

APATOSAURUS GROWTH RATE

It is difficult to tell how long a dinosaur lived. Sometimes, growth lines in the bones (like the rings of trees) suggest the animal grew more quickly at some time of each year. Its age can be assessed by counting the lines. Studies of the bones of *Apatosaurus* (previously known as *Brontosaurus*), the relative of *Diplodocus*, suggest that these sauropods grew quickly, without growth rings, for about 10 years. By then, they had reached 90 percent of their adult size. After they reached this age, they grew very little.

10 YEARS

BRACHIOSAURUS

Although many remains have been found in the Morrison Formation in the western United States, the most complete skeleton of *Brachiosaurus* was found halfway across the globe in Tanzania. This shows that in late Jurassic times Pangaea had not yet split up completely and the same types of dinosaur lived all over the world. A German expedition unearthed this skeleton in 1909, when Tanzania was still called German East Africa. The complete skeleton, the biggest mounted anywhere, is currently on display in the Humboldt Museum in Berlin, Germany as shown left.

TRIASSIC 245-208 MYA	EARLY/MID JURASSIC 208-157 MYA	LATE JURASSIC 157-146 MYA	EARLY CRETACEOUS 146-97 MYA	LATE CRETACEOUS 97-65 MYA

THE HEYDAY OF THE SAUROPODS

During the late Jurassic period, sauropods were at their most prolific and widespread. Some were long and low, and browsed the low vegetation. Others were tall and browsed the lower branches of trees. These two main types were distinguished by the shape of their teeth. *Diplodocus* and the other long, low sauropods had peg-like teeth; while the taller stouter sauropods, such as *Brachiosaurus*, had thick, spoon-shaped teeth which indicate a different type of feeding arrangement. However, nobody is yet sure what it was.

DINOSAUR DETECTIVES

Often, when the remains of a very big animal are discovered there are tantalizingly few bones found. Comparing them directly to a more complete skeleton can give us some idea of the kind of animal they came from. In 1999, four neck vertebrae of a gigantic sauropod turned up. The *Sauroposeidon* bones turned out to be very similar to the neck bones of *Brachiosaurus*. So, we are fairly sure *Sauroposeidon* was an animal very like *Brachiosaurus*—but much bigger!

SEISMOSAURUS

The longest dinosaur known is *Seismosaurus*. Imagine *Diplodocus*, then double its length. Make this length by stretching the neck and the tail in proportion to the body and this is what *Seismosaurus* looked like. So far, only one *Seismosaurus* skeleton has been found and that was in the Morrison Formation rocks in New Mexico. The skeleton is of an animal that may have been about 164 feet (50 m) long.

DRESSED TO IMPRESS

Not only did the late sauropods have armor, but some of them had strange spines and frills as well. *Amargasaurus* from early Cretaceous Argentina had a double row of spines down its neck and a tall fin down its back. Unusual sauropods developed in Cretaceous South America because it was an island continent at the time, and animals developed differently there.

ARGENTINOSAURUS

To date, the heaviest dinosaur ever found is *Argentinosaurus*. We have only six vertebrae, a part of its hips, a bit of rib and a leg bone. The leg bone is as tall as a man. From this we deduce the animal was about 88 feet (27 m) long and weighed about 55 tons (50 tonnes). A new grouping, the andesaurids, was set up for it. Like some earlier Morrison Formation sauropods, *Argentinosaurus* had vertebrae made of thin struts and sheets of bone with great hollows between them—a strong but light construction, vital for such a huge animal.

VERTEBRAE

LEGBONE

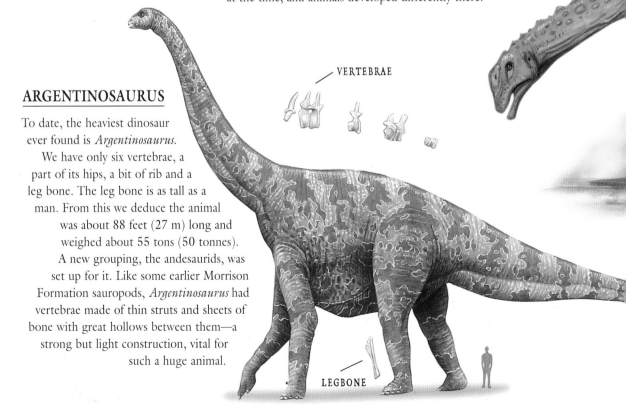

THE LAST OF THE SAUROPODS

As the world passed from the Jurassic into the Cretaceous period, the vegetation began to change and the continents to move apart. Different dinosaurs were becoming prominent. The sauropods began to die away as a completely different group of plant-eating dinosaurs developed. In some places the sauropods still thrived, either because the old style vegetation still flourished in some areas, or because they lived on isolated continents where the new dinosaurs did not reach. Despite the spread of the new dinosaur types there were sauropods existing right to the very end of the Dinosaur Age.

TOUGH GUY

The bony armor pieces from the back of a titanosaurid were found as long ago as 1890 in Madagascar. The palaeontologist who first identified them was not believed, as no other sauropod was known to be covered in armor. Only with the discovery of armored titanosaurids in Argentina in the 1970s and a more complete armored titanosaurid in Madagascar in the 1990s was this scientist's theory proven to be correct.

SALTASAURUS

Of the sauropods that survived into the Cretaceous period the titanosaurids (such as *Saltasaurus* in Argentina or *Ampelosaurus* in France) were perhaps the most successful. Despite their name, at about 39 feet (12 m) long, they were not particularly big for sauropods. In recent years, it has been found that at least some titanosaurids had a back covered in armor. This may not have been for defense but, like the shell on the back of a crab, it might have been for stiffening the backbone to help the animal carry its weight.

TRIASSIC	EARLY/MID JURASSIC	LATE JURASSIC	EARLY CRETACEOUS	LATE CRETACEOUS
245-208 MYA	208-157 MYA	157-146 MYA	146-97 MYA	97-65 MYA

ORNITHOPODS: THE BIRD FEET

HYPSILOPHODON SKULL

The skull of an ornithopod was different from that of a sauropod. There was always a beak at the front for cropping the food. The teeth were not merely for raking in leaves but were designed for chewing them, either by chopping or grinding. Depressions at each side of the skull show where there were probably cheek pouches, used to hold the food while it was being processed. This is a far more complicated arrangement than that of the prosauropods and sauropods.

During the Triassic period, at about the same time as the meat-eating dinosaurs and the prosauropods appeared, another group of plant-eating dinosaurs developed. What made these dinosaurs different was the arrangement of bones in the hip, which gave more space for the big gut needed by plant-eaters, yet enabled them to balance on their hind legs. As a result, most of these animals were two-footed herbivores. Victorian scientists called the long-necked plant-eaters the sauropods (lizard feet) because they had a lizard-like arrangement of bones in their feet; the two-footed, bird-hipped dinosaurs they called the ornithopods (bird feet). We still use these terms today.

ADVANCED JAWS

Later, more advanced ornithopods had quite complex chewing mechanisms. An animal like *Iguanodon* or a hadrosaur had its upper teeth mounted on articulated plates at each side of the skull. As the lower jaw rose these plates moved outwards to allow the sloping chewing surfaces of both sets of teeth to grind past one another. This constant milling action wore away the teeth, and new ones grew to replace them.

SAUROPOD

ORNITHOPOD

HIPBONES

As with the prosauropods the hipbones of the sauropods incorporated a pubic bone that pointed down and forward. This meant the big plant-digesting intestines had to be carried forward of the hips. In ornithopods this pubic bone is swept back, except for a pair of forward extensions that splayed out to the side. The big plant-digesting intestines could be carried beneath the animal's hipbone, closer to its center of gravity. This enabled the ornithopod to walk on its hind legs, balanced by its tail—just like a meat-eating dinosaur.

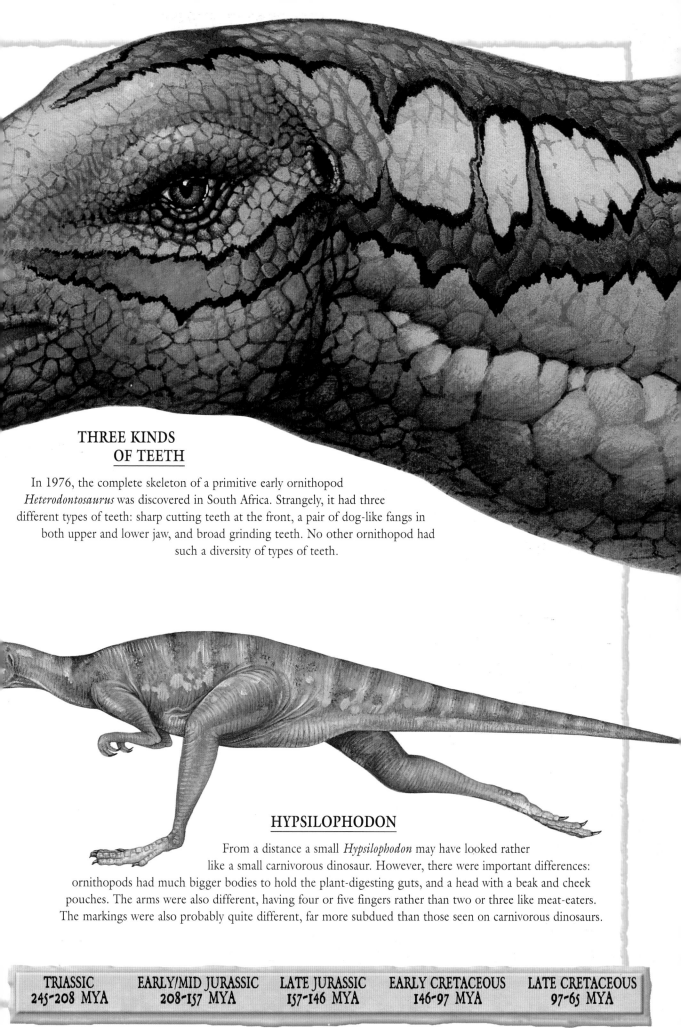

THREE KINDS
OF TEETH

In 1976, the complete skeleton of a primitive early ornithopod
Heterodontosaurus was discovered in South Africa. Strangely, it had three
different types of teeth: sharp cutting teeth at the front, a pair of dog-like fangs in
both upper and lower jaw, and broad grinding teeth. No other ornithopod had
such a diversity of types of teeth.

HYPSILOPHODON

From a distance a small *Hypsilophodon* may have looked rather
like a small carnivorous dinosaur. However, there were important differences:
ornithopods had much bigger bodies to hold the plant-digesting guts, and a head with a beak and cheek
pouches. The arms were also different, having four or five fingers rather than two or three like meat-eaters.
The markings were also probably quite different, far more subdued than those seen on carnivorous dinosaurs.

TRIASSIC	EARLY/MID JURASSIC	LATE JURASSIC	EARLY CRETACEOUS	LATE CRETACEOUS
245-208 MYA	208-157 MYA	157-146 MYA	146-97 MYA	97-65 MYA

CHANGING FACE

Over the years, as more specimens were found, scientists changed their opinions on what they thought *Iguanodon* looked like. In the 1850s, reconstructions of the beast were built in the Crystal Palace gardens, south London, along the lines of Mantell's big lizard. Then, in 1878, a whole herd of *Iguanodon* skeletons, mostly complete, were found in a coal mine in Bernissart, Belgium. These animals were up to 33 feet (10 m) long and had hind legs that were much longer than their forelimbs. This evidence led to new reconstructions of *Iguanodon* sitting on its hind legs like a kangaroo—an image that became accepted for the next century.

IGUANA TOOTH

The first remains of *Iguanodon*—teeth and parts of bones—were discovered in Kent, England in about 1822 by English country doctor Gideon Mantell and his wife Mary. Other scientists of the day thought they were the teeth of fish, or of a hippopotamus. But Mantell realized the teeth were from a plant-eating reptile like a modern iguana lizard. His first reconstructions showed a kind of a dragon-sized, iguana-like reptile, similar to the first reconstructions of the meat-eating *Megalosaurus*, also recently discovered.

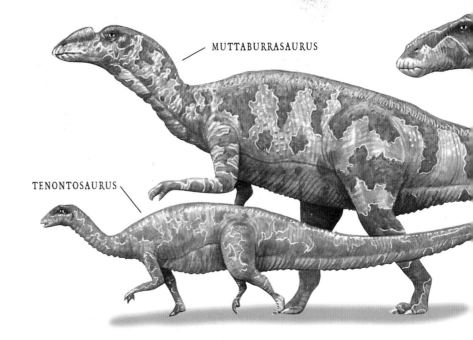

MUTTABURRASAURUS

TENONTOSAURUS

THE OURANOSAURUS QUESTION

One iguanodontid, *Ouranosaurus*, had an arrangement of tall spines forming a kind of a wicket fence along its backbone, probably to support some sort of fin or sail. As *Ouranosaurus* lived in North Africa, which was hot and arid during Cretaceous times, such a sail could have regulated its body temperature by exposing blood vessels to the warming Sun and cooling wind. A meat-eater, *Spinosaurus*, lived in the same time and place and also had a sail. Another theory is that the spines supported a fatty hump, such as camels have today.

THE IGUANODON DYNASTY

*I*guanodon was among the first dinosaurs to be discovered. Its remains came to light about the same time as those of the meat-eater *Megalosaurus*. The teeth and a few scraps of bone were found first and were obviously from a very large plant-eating reptile. At the time, few people were familiar with modern plant-eating reptiles, so the animal was particularly unusual. Some scientific work was being done on the modern South American plant-eating lizard, the iguana, which had teeth rather like those of this new fossil. Hence, it was given the name, *Iguanodon*.

IGUANODON

GASPARINISAURA

MEET THE FAMILY

The modern interpretation of *Iguanodon* is that, as an adult, it was too heavy to spend much time on its hind legs, so went about mostly on all fours. Since it was discovered, scientists have found many more closely-related iguanodontids. Australian *Muttaburrasaurus* was slightly smaller and had a high ridge on its nose. American *Tenontosaurus* had a particularly long tail. The most primitive member of the group was *Gasparinisaura* from Argentina, which was only the size of a turkey. All of them had lived during the Cretaceous period.

IGUANODON FOOD

Iguanodon lived in northern Europe during early Cretaceous times. It wandered in herds across swampy landscapes, knee-deep in reed-beds of horsetail plants that grew just like our modern species. The herds probably grazed on these horsetails as they moved from one area to another.

TRIASSIC 245-208 MYA	EARLY/MID JURASSIC 208-157 MYA	LATE JURASSIC 157-146 MYA	EARLY CRETACEOUS 146-97 MYA	LATE CRETACEOUS 97-65 MYA

THE DUCKBILLS

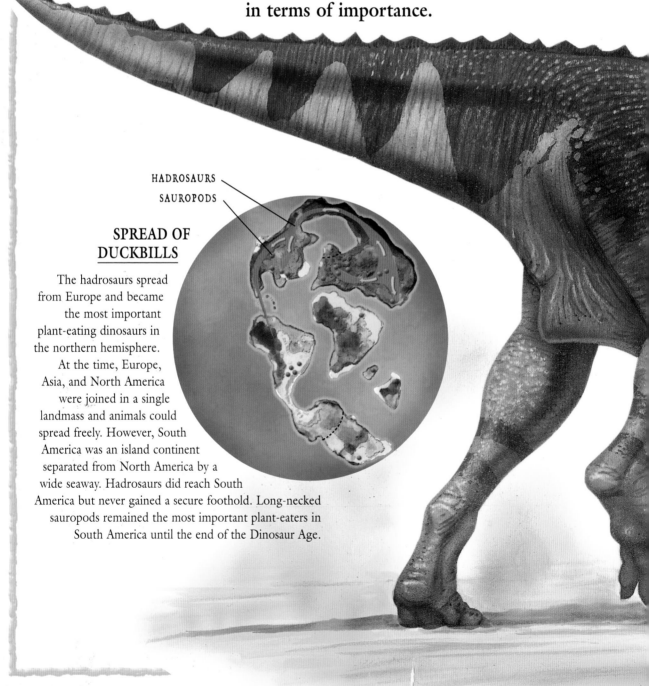

I n the later Cretaceous period, a new group of ornithopods developed from the iguanodontids. The vegetation was changing: primitive forests were giving way to modern-looking woodlands of oak, beech, and other broad-leaved trees as well as clusters of conifers and undergrowths of flowering herbs. These new dinosaurs, the hadrosaurs, spread and flourished in the broad-leaved forests throughout Europe, Asia, and North America. They had thousands of grinding teeth and the front of the mouth supported a broad beak. These dinosaurs took over from the sauropods in terms of importance.

HADROSAURS

SAUROPODS

SPREAD OF DUCKBILLS

The hadrosaurs spread from Europe and became the most important plant-eating dinosaurs in the northern hemisphere.

At the time, Europe, Asia, and North America were joined in a single landmass and animals could spread freely. However, South America was an island continent separated from North America by a wide seaway. Hadrosaurs did reach South America but never gained a secure foothold. Long-necked sauropods remained the most important plant-eaters in South America until the end of the Dinosaur Age.

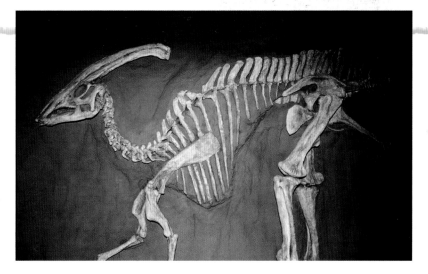

HEAD CRESTS

Some hadrosaurs, such as this *Parasaurolophus*, were quite striking because of their elaborate head crests. Mostly made of hollow bone connected to the nostrils, they were probably used for making noises to signal to one another through dense forests. Each type of hadrosaur had a unique crest shape, so that different herds could be distinguished from one another. Those with flat heads or solid crests probably supported an inflatable flap of skin that could have been puffed up like a frog's throat to make a noise.

MODERN CONIFERS

Modern conifers, such as pine and spruce, as well as the broad-leaved trees, such as oak and ash, appeared in Cretaceous times. Until then, more primitive conifers, such as monkey puzzle trees, had sustained the sauropods. Hadrosaurs were well-equipped for dealing with the new conifer trees. They used their broad beaks to scrape off the needles and their batteries of teeth to grind them down before swallowing.

HADROSAURUS

Hadrosaurus was, like *Iguanodon*, essentially a two-footed plant-eating dinosaur that would have been rather too heavy to spend much time on its hind legs as an adult. It would have moved about on all fours, a theory confirmed by the fleshy weight-bearing pads it had on its forelimbs. *Hadrosaurus'* tail was very deep and flat which once led scientists to think the hadrosaur may have been a swimming animal—an idea that has now been discarded. Its most distinctive feature, was its broad, flat, duck-like beak.

TRIASSIC	EARLY/MID JURASSIC	LATE JURASSIC	EARLY CRETACEOUS	LATE CRETACEOUS
245-208 MYA	208-157 MYA	157-146 MYA	146-97 MYA	97-65 MYA

DEATH OF DENVER STEGOSAURUS

A team from the Denver Museum discovered a stegosaurus skeleton
by accident while excavating another dinosaur. This *Stegosaurus* had a
diseased tail after a broken tail spike became infected. The weakened animal
then died during a drought. Its internal organs rotted and its stomach
bloated, rolling it over on to its back. The drought ended and a nearby river
burst its banks, covering the *Stegosaurus* with silt. All this was deduced
140 million years later from the fossil and the types of rocks found nearby.
Such study of the lead-up to fossilization is known as "taphonomy."

STEGOSAURUS

Stegosaurus lived in North America at the end of the
Jurassic period. We know it was a big four-footed animal,
up to 26 feet (8 m) long, with shorter legs at the front.
A double row of plates stuck up along its back, and two pairs
of spikes stuck out on either side towards the tip of its tail.
It had a very small head and a kind of armored mesh
protected its throat. Some scientists
think the plates were covered in horn and
formed an armored shield. Others insist
the plates were covered in skin and acted
as heat exchangers. On cool days, they
absorbed warmth, while on hot days, the
animal could have cooled its blood by
turning the plates into
the wind.

THE BRAINS OF
THE FAMILY?

The head of a *Stegosaurus* was
particularly small and held a
very small brain. As
with ornithopods
and their relatives it
had a beak at the
front of the mouth
and probably cheeks
along the side.

TRIASSIC 245-208 MYA	EARLY/MID JURASSIC 208-157 MYA	LATE JURASSIC 157-146 MYA	EARLY CRETACEOUS 146-97 MYA	LATE CRETACEOUS 97-65 MYA

THE PLATED LIZARDS

Not long after the ornithopods came into existence, all kinds of other dinosaurs began to develop from them. Many of these dinosaurs sported armor of one kind or another, and they were too heavy to spend much time on two legs. They became mostly four-footed beasts. One of the groups had armor arranged in a double row of plates or spikes down its back and tail. These plated dinosaurs were known as stegosaurs.

FLAT   PAIRS

SINGLE OVERLAPPING ROW   DOUBLE ALTERNATING

UNDER ATTACK

PLATE PUZZLES

The back plates of *Stegosaurus* were embedded in its skin but not attached directly to its skeleton. This has caused uncertainty about how they were arranged. One theory suggests the plates lay flat as armor along the animal's back. Another is that they stood upright in pairs. Yet another says they had a single upright row of overlapping plates. The most widely accepted view is that they stood in a double row, alternating with one another. Some scientists suggest the muscles at the base of the plates would have allowed *Stegosaurus* to point them at an attacker.

CLEVER TAIL

Most stegosaurids had two pairs of spikes at the end of their tail. The tails were usually quite flexible and could have been swung sideways with some force against the flanks of an attacker. There was a gap in the hipbones that may have held a concentration of nerves to control the hind legs and tail, and a gland that supplied extra energy. This space in the tail gave rise to a once-popular misconception that stegosaurids had a second brain controlling their tails.

A WORLD OF STEGOSAURIDS

Stegosaurus was not the only stegosaurid. There were many others, ranging from North America, through Europe to Asia. They probably developed from an early Jurassic group called the scelidosurids. The most primitive of the stegosaurids we know were found in middle Jurassic rocks in China. From such medium-sized animals developed the wide range of plated and spiked dinosaurs that were important in late Jurassic times. By the middle Cretaceous they had all but died out. The remains of an animal that may have been a stegosaurid was found in late Cretaceous rocks in India. Perhaps the group lasted longer in India which was an island continent at the time. Or perhaps the specimen was wrongly identified. Scientists are still not sure.

KENTROSAURUS

56

EAST AFRICAN DISCOVERIES

The Humboldt Museum in Berlin, Germany has a collection of late Jurassic dinosaurs excavated from East Africa in the 1920s. Among them are the stegosaurid *Kentrosaurus*, which was very similar to the North American *Stegosaurus*. There were also sauropods such as *Dicraeosaurus* (shown left), which was similar to *Diplodocus*.

AN EARLY STEGOSAURID

Cow-sized *Scelidosaurus*, known from the early Jurassic rocks of England, was a four-footed herbivore covered in small studs of armor. It may have been an ancestor of the stegosaurids; or of the later Cretaceous nodosaurids of America, and the middle Jurassic to late Cretaceous ankylosaurids of Europe, North America, and Asia. It may even have been ancestral to both.

VARIETY OF STEGOSAURIDS

The most primitive stegosaurid known is 13-feet (4-m) long *Huayangosaurus* from middle Jurassic China. Later stegosaurids had shorter front legs than hind, but those of *Huayangosaurus* hardly varied. Its armor included paired narrow back spikes and a tail with two pairs of spikes. It also had a pair of shoulder spikes, as did some later stegosaurids. *Dacenturus* from late Jurassic Europe had low rounded plates on its shoulders and back, and tall spikes all down its tail. Late Jurassic *Kentrosaurus* from Africa had its center of gravity at its hips, so, like some sauropods, it could rise on its hind legs to browse (as could *Stegosaurus*). *Wuerhosaurus* from early Cretaceous China was as big as *Stegosaurus* and had long low back plates.

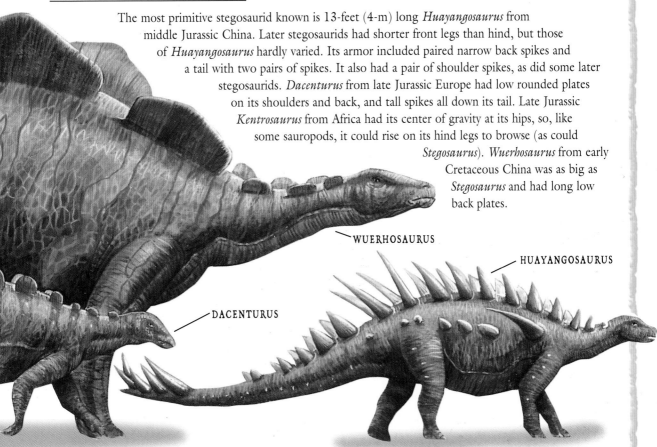

WUERHOSAURUS

HUAYANGOSAURUS

DACENTURUS

TRIASSIC 245-208 MYA	EARLY/MID JURASSIC 208-157 MYA	LATE JURASSIC 157-146 MYA	EARLY CRETACEOUS 146-97 MYA	LATE CRETACEOUS 97-65 MYA

THE NODOSAURIDS: SPIKY DINOSAURS

As the Jurassic period passed, the armored stegosaurids became extinct and other groups of armored dinosaurs developed. The two most closely related groups were the nodosaurids and the ankylosaurids. Each had small bony plates across their broad backs. These plates stretched up the neck to the head and down the tail, and would have had horny covers that made the animal's back impregnable. The distinctive feature of the nodosaurid group was the presence of long robust spikes sticking out sideways and upwards from the shoulders and from the sides.

GASTONIA

One of the best-preserved nodosaurid fossils ever found was that of *Gastonia*. Its armor was tightly-packed, forming a solid shield over its hips. Spikes stood up over the shoulders, and it had a series of broad flat spines, almost like blades, sticking outwards and running down each side from its neck to its tail. It was found in early Cretaceous rocks in Utah, USA, but an almost identical early Cretaceous dinosaur has been found in England.

SPIKY CUSTOMERS

Two related groups of armored dinosaur existed in Cretaceous times. The nodosaurids were characterized by spikes on the neck and sides, while the ankylosaurids had clubs on the ends of their tails.

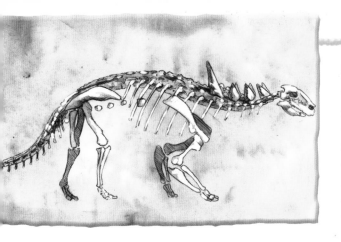

SAUROPELTA SKELETON

The solid back plate armor is the most commonly fossilized part of a nodosaurid, and is usually found upside-down. If a nodosaurid died and fell into a river, it may have been washed out to sea. As it decayed, expanding digestive gases in its gut would have turned it over, its heavy back acting as a keel. As it settled on the sea bed, it would be buried and eventually fossilized in that position.

STRUTHIOSAURUS

Not all nodosaurids were big animals. *Struthiosaurus* from late Cretaceous rocks of central Europe was only 6 ½ feet (2 m) long, with a body the size of a dog. It appears to have been an island-dweller. Animals tend to develop into smaller forms on islands to make the best use of the limited food stocks. A modern example would be the tiny Shetland pony from the islands off Scotland.

SAUROPELTA

One of the earliest known nodosaurids was *Sauropelta* from Montana and Wyoming, USA. It had an arched back, long tail, and hind legs that were longer than its fore legs. Like all other nodosaurids its neck, back, and tail were covered in armor. *Sauropelta's* long defensive spines were confined to its neck and shoulders, and spread outwards and upwards. At 16 feet (5 m) long, *Sauropelta* was an average size for a nodosaurid.

TRIASSIC 245-208 MYA	EARLY/MID JURASSIC 208-157 MYA	LATE JURASSIC 157-146 MYA	EARLY CRETACEOUS 146-97 MYA	LATE CRETACEOUS 97-65 MYA

EUOPLOCEPHALUS

The best known of the ankylosaurids is *Euoplocephalus*, 16 feet (5 m) long and living a little earlier than *Ankylosaurus* in Alberta, Canada. Its back was an articulated mass of armor, the head an armored box. Even its eyelids were armored and slammed shut like the steel shutters of a battleship whenever danger approached. Scientists think it used its powerful club tail to repel attacks from even the most intimidating of predators, such as this *Tyrannosaurus rex*.

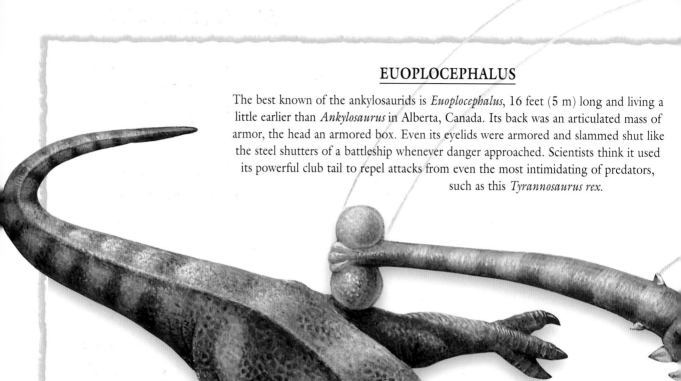

TAIL CLUB

The tail of *Euoplocephalus* and other ankylosaurids had a heavy club at the end. To support it the vertebrae of half the tail were fused together in a solid bar, making it like the shaft of a medieval mace. The muscles at the broad hips and the flexible part of the base of the tail would have allowed this club to be swung sideways with great force against the legs and flanks of a raiding meat-eating dinosaur, breaking bones and crippling the attacker for life.

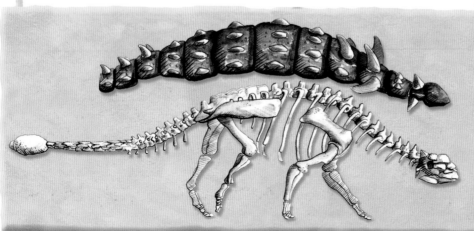

A LOT OF GUTS

Without its armor we can see that *Euoplocephalus* was a heavy four-footed animal. Its hips were broad but the design allowed the guts to be carried well back. The guts would have been massive and probably contained fermenting chambers like those of modern cows.

THE ANKYLOSAURIDS: THE CLUB-TAILS

The ankylosaurids were closely related to the nodosaurids but mostly came later, towards the end of the Cretaceous period. With their armored necks and backs, they looked very like their relatives but instead of having spikes on the shoulders and the sides they had a different weapon—a heavy bony club at the end of the tail. This could have been devastating when swung at an enemy. It is also possible that the club may have been used as a decoy. Perhaps the club on the tail looked like a head on a neck, and caused meat-eaters to attack it instead of the more vulnerable front end.

CRETACEOUS UNDERGROWTH

By the end of the Cretaceous period, modern plants had developed. Beneath the broad-leaved trees was an undergrowth of flowering herbs such as buttercups. The ankylosaurids and the nodosaurids carried their heads low and their mouths close to the ground. They were evidently low-level feeders that ate the flowering herbs.

TRIASSIC 245-208 MYA	EARLY/MID JURASSIC 208-157 MYA	LATE JURASSIC 157-146 MYA	EARLY CRETACEOUS 146-97 MYA	LATE CRETACEOUS 97-65 MYA

HEADS

Each group of pachycephalosaurids had its own type of skull shape and ornamentation. *Stegoceras* and *Homalocephale*, both from Mongolia, had sloping heads, higher at the rear, the latter with an elaborate head crest. *Prenocephale*, also from Mongolia, had a more rounded dome-like head. Both had decorative lumps around the bony crown. North-American *Stygimoloch* was perhaps the strangest, with a weird array of spikes and spines all around its dome. These were probably used for intimidation rather than fighting. All pachycephalosaurids lived in the late Cretaceous era.

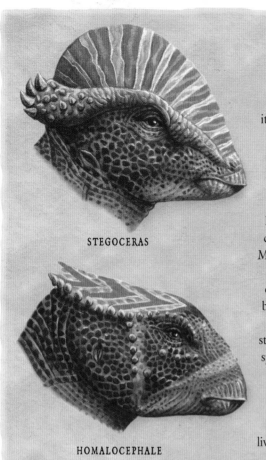

STEGOCERAS

HOMALOCEPHALE

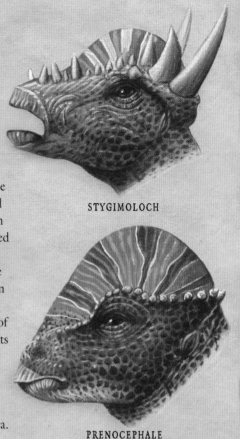

STYGIMOLOCH

PRENOCEPHALE

MODERN SPARRERS

In the American Rocky Mountains, modern bighorn sheep and mountain goats go through an annual ritual in which the males fight the flock leader to test his strength. The construction of their skulls and horns protects them from suffering much damage when they bash against one another. Pachycephalosaurids probably had similar rituals.

TRIASSIC 245-208 MYA	EARLY/MID JURASSIC 208-157 MYA	LATE JURASSIC 157-146 MYA	EARLY CRETACEOUS 146-97 MYA	LATE CRETACEOUS 97-65 MYA

BONEHEADS

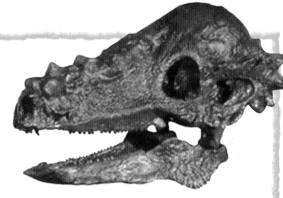

Imagine a dinosaur, a two-footed plant-eating dinosaur such as an ornithopod, but give it a very high forehead so that it looks brainy. What you would have is a pachycephalosaurid—another dinosaur group descended from the ornithopods. The intelligent look is misleading. The brain in that head is tiny and the roof of the skull is made up of very thick bone. Scientists think the mass of bone on top of the head was used as a weapon—a kind of battering ram. This was probably not for use against predators but for display purposes in courtship battles.

ALL CREATURES GREAT AND SMALL

There was a great range of sizes in pachycephalosaurids. The largest known, at 16 feet (5 m) long, was the North American *Pachycephalosaurus*. The smallest was *Micropachycephalosaurus* from China, which was about the size of a rabbit. This smallest pachycephalosaurid has the longest dinosaur name ever given.

HORNED BATTLERS

The most complete pachycephalosaurid known is *Stegoceras*. The grain of its head bone and the strength of its neck probably provided an awesome degree of protection. They seem to have lived in herds. The adult males probably fought with one another to be the leader of the herd; the strongest of them would then mate with the females.

HARD HEADS

Dinosaur skulls are rarely preserved as fossils, but pachycephalosaurid skulls were different. The top bone of the skull was so massive it often survived as a fossil. Commonly, the only part of the animal to be preserved, these skulls are often found very battered. This suggests they were washed down a river for long distances before being buried in sediment. This may mean they were mountain-living animals, like their modern counterparts—mountain sheep.

THE PRIMITIVE-HORNED DINOSAURS

The last of the plant-eating dinosaur groups existed from the mid to late Cretaceous period. Like the ankylosaurids and the nodosaurids they lived in North America and in Asia, and they also developed from ornithopods. They were equipped with armor but it was confined solely to the head. Early types were lightly-built and very ornithopod-like, but in later forms the armor on the head became so heavy they went about as four-footed animals. Flamboyant neck shields and horns developed and these horned dinosaurs became known as the ceratopsians.

AN EARLY SHEEP

Scientists regard *Protoceratops* as the sheep of late Cretaceous Mongolia. Similar in size, they lived in herds and grazed the sparse vegetation of the arid landscape. One particular *Protoceratops* fossil had the remains of a fierce carnivore, *Velociraptor*, clinging to its head shield. The meat-eater had attacked the ceratopsian with its killing claws, but the ceratopsian must have fought back with its big beak as both dinosaurs lost their lives during the fight.

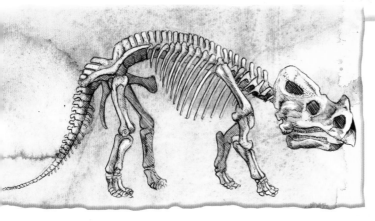

BIG BROTHER

By the time *Montanoceratops* had developed, towards the end of the late Cretaceous, the ceratopsians were bigger and had developed the horns on their head. *Montanoceratops* was about 10 feet (3 m) long and walked on all fours. However, like its two-footed ancestors, it still had claws on its feet. In later ceratopsians the toenails developed into hooves, better able to take the weight of big animals.

ARCHAEOCERATOPS

The most primitive of the ceratopsians known is *Archaeoceratops*. It was a very small animal, about 3 feet (1 m) long, and scampered nimbly on hind legs about the plains of late Cretaceous China. It had a head that was very similar to that of *Psittacosaurus*. Its skeleton was so primitive and generalized it is possible that its descendants gave rise to the big ceratopsians that were to follow.

WHO'S A PRETTY BOY?

An early relative of the ceratopsians was the 5 feet (1.5 m) long parrot-lizard *Psittacosaurus*. It developed a very strong beak and powerful jaws for plucking and chopping the tough vegetation it ate. A bony ridge around the back of the skull anchored its strong jaw muscles. The bony ridge and its big beak gave its skull a square shape, and the head must have looked very like the big-beaked head of a modern parrot.

CYCAD FOSSIL

At the end of the Cretaceous period the old-style vegetation was largely replaced by modern species of plants. However, some of the older types of palm-like cycads remained in some regions. In the areas where they occurred, the ceratopsians may have relied on these plants. Their narrow beaks would have reached into the palm-like clump of fronds and selected the best pieces, and their strong jaws would have shredded the tough leaves.

TRIASSIC	EARLY/MID JURASSIC	LATE JURASSIC	EARLY CRETACEOUS	LATE CRETACEOUS
245-208 MYA	208-157 MYA	157-146 MYA	146-97 MYA	97-65 MYA

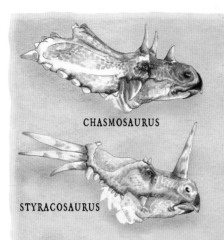

CHASMOSAURUS

STYRACOSAURUS

VARIETY OF HEADS

Ceratopsians all had the same body shape, but their different shapes of shield and horn arrangements made each type easily recognizable to their own herd. *Styracosaurus* had a monumental horn on its nose and an array of horns around its shield. *Chasmosaurus* had an enormous, sail-like shield. *Einiosaurus* had a long nose horn that curved forwards and a pair of straight horns at the edge of its shield. *Acheluosaurus* had a battering ram on its nose, a pair of short, blade-like horns above its eyes, and a curved pair at the shield-edge.

ALL FOR ONE

The horns of ceratopsians would have been used to defend themselves and their herd against big carnivores and also to tussle with one another over position in the herd. Having locked horns, they would have pushed and shoved until one of them gave way. Little harm would have come to the loser. While traveling, the ceratopsians may have kept their young at the center of the herd to protect them. If attacked by carnivores they may have formed a circle with the youngsters in the center and the adults facing outwards so that the attackers were faced with the shields and horns of all the herd. Today, musk-oxen protect their herd in this way.

WILDEBEEST

We know ceratopsians moved about in herds because we have found bone beds consisting of many hundreds, even thousands, of skeletons. The animals would have been migrating, traveling in herds to areas where there was more food at a particular time of year. When crossing a river they may have been caught by a sudden flash flood that washed them away and dumped their bodies. This still happens in Africa today as herds of wildebeest migrate from one feeding ground to another.

THE BIG-HORNED DINOSAURS

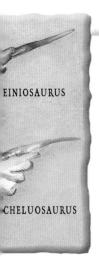

EINIOSAURUS

CHELUOSAURUS

The big ceratopsians were probably the most spectacular dinosaurs of the late Cretaceous period. They were all four-footed animals, mostly as big as today's rhinoceros. The ridge of bone around the neck had developed into a broad shield. They also had an array of long horns on their face. The skulls of the big ceratopsians were so solid and tough that they were often preserved as fossils. As a result, we know a lot about their heads. There were two main sub-groups. One developed long frills and a pair of long horns above the eyes; the other had shorter frills and tended to have a single horn on the nose.

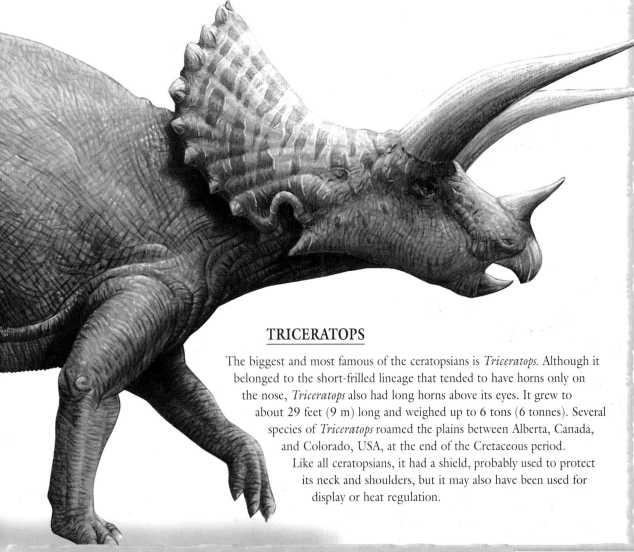

TRICERATOPS

The biggest and most famous of the ceratopsians is *Triceratops*. Although it belonged to the short-frilled lineage that tended to have horns only on the nose, *Triceratops* also had long horns above its eyes. It grew to about 29 feet (9 m) long and weighed up to 6 tons (6 tonnes). Several species of *Triceratops* roamed the plains between Alberta, Canada, and Colorado, USA, at the end of the Cretaceous period. Like all ceratopsians, it had a shield, probably used to protect its neck and shoulders, but it may also have been used for display or heat regulation.

TRIASSIC 245-208 MYA	EARLY/MID JURASSIC 208-157 MYA	LATE JURASSIC 157-146 MYA	EARLY CRETACEOUS 146-97 MYA	LATE CRETACEOUS 97-65 MYA

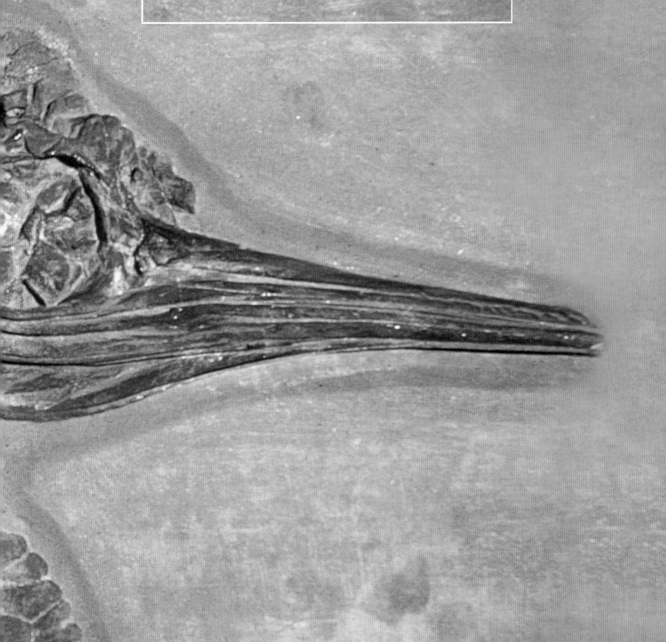

IN THE SEA

A RETRO-PIONEER

Spinoaequalis was the earliest-known land animal to re-adapt itself to a water-living existence. It was a lizard-like beast found in late Carboniferous marine sediments of Kansas in the United States. Its name means "equal spine," which refers to the strong spines on the tail that made a flat vertical paddle and allowed for the attachment of strong muscles—in short, the tail of a swimming animal. The rest of the skeleton is that of a land-living creature.

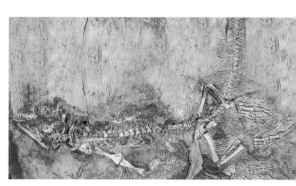

A FRESHWATER PUZZLE

Mesosaurus was a freshwater reptile, about 3 feet (1 m) long, with a flattened swimming tail and powerful webbed hind legs. It probably used its tail and hind legs to drive itself through the water, steering and stabilizing itself with its webbed front feet. Its teeth were fine and needle-like and were probably used for filtering invertebrates from the water to eat. The odd thing about it, though, is the fact that its skeletons are found in early Permian rocks in both South Africa and Brazil. Scientists wondered how the remains of a freshwater animal were fossilized on two widely separated continents. It was the first piece of evidence in support of a revolutionary concept called "plate tectonics."

THE PROOF OF DRIFT

In Permian times, when *Mesosaurus* was alive, there was no Atlantic Ocean. What is now Africa and South America were part of a single vast landmass call Pangaea. The same kinds of animal lived all over the world because there were no oceans to separate them. The presence of the skeleton of *Mesosaurus* in both South Africa and Brazil was one of the first pieces of evidence put forward to support the theory that continents drift apart over time—also known as "plate tectonics."

THE FIRST SWIMMERS

All life came from the sea. Scientists estimate that life appeared about 3,500 million years ago, and only relatively recently did it come out on to land (about 400 million years ago for plants and 300 million years ago for animals). Some of the first land creatures developed into reptiles and the dinosaurs. Almost as soon as land life had become established, some apparently returned to the sea to exploit new food sources. As early as 250 million years ago, there were water-living animals that appear to have developed from land-living ancestors even before the dinosaurs.

A MODERN EXAMPLE

The Galapagos marine iguana looks and lives very much like some of these early swimming reptiles. It has adopted a partially aquatic way of life because it feeds on seaweed. Its lizard body, legs, and feet show that it is a land-living animal, but its muscular, flexible tail is ideal for swimming. It also has the ability to hold its breath for long periods and a method for removing excess salt absorbed from the seawater from its system. These are adaptations that wouldn't show up in fossils, so we do not know if early swimming reptiles had them or not.

THE BUOYANCY PROBLEM

Hovasaurus from late Permian rocks found in Madagascar had a swimming tail twice the length of the rest of its body. It was so long that it would have been difficult to use on land. However the feet were those of a land-living reptile. Most skeletons of *Hovasaurus* have pebbles lying in the stomach area. Evidently this animal swallowed stones to adjust its buoyancy underwater. This is one of the swimming techniques used by animals whose ancestors were land-living animals.

CARBONIFEROUS 360-286 MYA	PERMIAN 286-245 MYA	TRIASSIC 245-208 MYA	EARLY/MID JURASSIC 208-157 MYA	LATE JURASSIC 157-146 MYA

LIFE AFTER DEATH

The science of "taphonomy" deals with what happens to an animal after it dies, and how it becomes a fossil. At sea this can be relatively simple.

1. When an animal dies it may float at the surface for a while until the gases generated in its decaying tissues disperse.

2. Eventually, however, it sinks to the bottom of the sea. A less buoyant animal may go straight to the bottom. There it may be scavengend by bottom-living creatures, and its parts broken up and dispersed.

3. If sand and mud are being deposited rapidly on the sea bed the body is quickly buried before too much damage is done.

4. After millions of years the sand and mud will be compressed and cemented together as rock, and the bones of the dead animal will have been replaced by minerals. It will have become a fossil.

A MODERN TURTLE

The turtle is a slow-moving aquatic reptile, shelled above and below, with paddle limbs that allow it to move through the water with a flying action. Protected from its enemies and surrounded by sources of food, it does not need speed or a streamlined shape to thrive.

AN EARLY WINNER

A broad body shape is adequate for a slow-moving animal, but such a creature remains vulnerable to attack from predators. This threat encouraged the development of armor in aquatic reptiles. The end result was the turtle. The earliest turtle, *Proganochelys*, dates from the late Triassic period, and lived in Germany. Its body shape and the arrangement of the shell is very similar to the modern turtle, which has not developed much in 215 million years.

BIG IS BEAUTIFUL

Archelon, the biggest turtle ever known, cruised the inland sea that covered much of North America in late Cretaceous times. At almost 13 feet (4 m) long it was bigger than a rowing boat. Its shell was reduced to a system of bony struts covered by tough skin; much like the biggest of the modern turtles, the leatherback. It probably fed on soft things like jellyfish, as just like the modern leatherback, its jaws were not very strong.

A SHOAL OF SWIMMING REPTILES

We have a good record of water-living animals because in an environment where sediment is constantly accumulating, these creatures have a better chance of being fossilized. From these fossils, we know that many of the sea creatures were in fact reptiles that had left dry land for a new life in the water. If there was more food in the water than on land, and if there were fewer dangerous predators in the sea, an aquatic life would have become enticing. Reptiles can adapt quite easily to such a lifestyle. They have a low metabolic rate and they can cope without oxygen for some time. In addition, moving around in the water takes only about a quarter of the energy of moving about on land.

BASILOSAURUS (WHALE)

MOSASAURUS (MOSASAUR)

METRIORHYNCHUS (CROCODILE)

CYMBOSPONDYLUS (ICHTHYOSAUR)

ZYGORHIZA (WHALE)

DOLICHORHYNCHOPS (PLESIOSAUR)

BAPTANODON (ICHTHYOSAUR)

DELPHINOSAURUS (ICHTHYOSAUR)

AN IDEAL SHAPE

The best shape for an underwater hunter is a streamlined body with a strong flattened tail and paddle limbs. Many of the Permian, Triassic, Jurassic, and Cretaceous swimming reptiles were built like this as were the tertiary whales. Some had strange adaptations like long necks that probably enabled them to reach prey hiding in rocks.

TRIASSIC 245-208 MYA	EARLY/MID JURASSIC 208-157 MYA	LATE JURASSIC 157-146 MYA	EARLY CRETACEOUS 146-97 MYA	LATE CRETACEOUS 97-65 MYA

PLACODONTS: THE SHELL-SEEKERS

PLACODUS

The most typical of the placodonts was *Placodus* itself. In appearance it looked rather like an enormous newt, about 7 feet (2 m) long, with a chunky body, a paddle-shaped tail, webbed feet and a short head.

There are all kinds of reasons why water-living animals should develop from land-living animals. Most persuasive of these is the idea that when a good food supply exists, then nature will develop something to exploit it. Shellfish represent one such food supply. The earliest group of reptiles that seemed to be particularly well adapted to feeding on shellfish were the placodonts. Although they still needed to come to the surface to breathe, they rooted about on the bed of the Tethys Sea that spread across southern Europe in Triassic times.

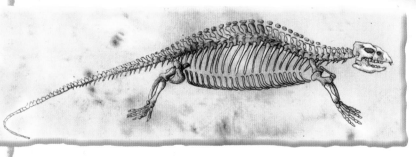

BUILT FOR BUOYANCY

A glimpse of the skeleton of *Placodus* reveals one of its main adaptations to its underwater way of life—"pachystosis." This means that the bones were broad and heavy, perfect for feeding on the bottom of the ocean. Animals that have pachystosis also have big lungs to help to regulate their buoyancy. To accommodate its huge lungs, *Placodus* developed a broad rib cage. A modern animal with these adaptations is the sea otter. Its weight and large lung capacity enable it to walk along the sea bed with ease, hunting shellfish. *Placodus* would have had the same lifestyle.

TRIASSIC 245-208 MYA	EARLY/MID JURASSIC 208-157 MYA	LATE JURASSIC 157-146 MYA	EARLY CRETACEOUS 146-97 MYA	LATE CRETACEOUS 97-65 MYA

PSEPHODERMA

HENODUS

PLACOCHELYS

MODERN EQUIVALENT

The walrus is a modern sea animal that eats shellfish. Its two great tusks are used for prising shellfish from rocks and it has crushing teeth at the back of its mouth. The tusks are also used as ice picks and for mating displays. We do not know if the protruding teeth of the placodonts had similar functions.

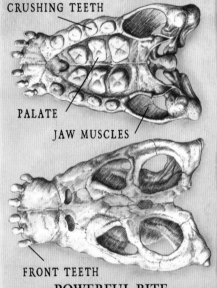

CRUSHING TEETH

PALATE

JAW MUSCLES

FRONT TEETH

POWERFUL BITE

From below, the protruding front teeth of *Placodus* are obvious. These were used for plucking the shells from the rocks and the seafloor. Further back the jaws have strong crushing teeth, and even the palate has a pavement of broad flat teeth, all ideal for smashing up the shells of shellfish. Holes in the side of the skull show where very powerful jaw muscles were attached. *Placodus* would have eaten bivalves such as mussels, scallops and oysters, similar to those that survive today, and brachiopods.

A SHELLED FAMILY

Because they were slow moving animals, the placodonts must have been very vulnerable to the meat-eaters of the time. Many developed shells on their backs as protection. In some types, the shells were extensive and looked very much like those of turtles, but the two groups of animals were in no way related. The similar shells developed independently among animals that had the same lifestyle in the same environment.

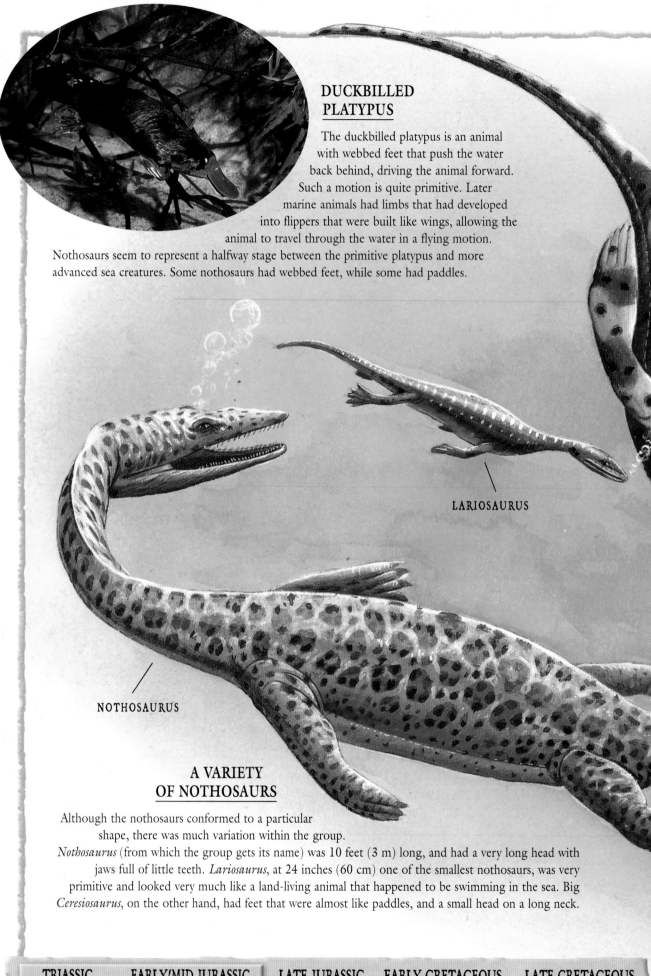

DUCKBILLED PLATYPUS

The duckbilled platypus is an animal
with webbed feet that push the water
back behind, driving the animal forward.
Such a motion is quite primitive. Later
marine animals had limbs that had developed
into flippers that were built like wings, allowing the
animal to travel through the water in a flying motion.
Nothosaurs seem to represent a halfway stage between the primitive platypus and more
advanced sea creatures. Some nothosaurs had webbed feet, while some had paddles.

LARIOSAURUS

NOTHOSAURUS

A VARIETY OF NOTHOSAURS

Although the nothosaurs conformed to a particular
shape, there was much variation within the group.
Nothosaurus (from which the group gets its name) was 10 feet (3 m) long, and had a very long head with
jaws full of little teeth. *Lariosaurus*, at 24 inches (60 cm) one of the smallest nothosaurs, was very
primitive and looked very much like a land-living animal that happened to be swimming in the sea. Big
Ceresiosaurus, on the other hand, had feet that were almost like paddles, and a small head on a long neck.

TRIASSIC 245-208 MYA	EARLY/MID JURASSIC 208-157 MYA	LATE JURASSIC 157-146 MYA	EARLY CRETACEOUS 146-97 MYA	LATE CRETACEOUS 97-65 MYA

BETWEEN THE LAND & THE SEA

The nothosaurs preceeded the plesiosaurs, rulers of the late Jurassic and Cretaceous seas. Like the placodonts, they are known mostly from remains found in the the the sediments laid down in the Tethys Sea, an ancient ocean that lay in the position where the Mediterranean Sea occupies today. Their necks, bodies, and tails were long and they had webbed feet (although they could still walk on land). Their hind limbs were larger than their front limbs and were used mostly for swimming. They had many small pointed teeth in long narrow jaws for catching fish. Nothosaurs seem to represent a part-way stage between land-living animals and fish-eating sea-going ones like the plesiosaurs.

LET'S GO FISHING

The long jaws and sharp teeth of *Nothosaurus* were ideal for catching fish. The long neck would have been able to reach fast-swimming fish quickly, and the little teeth would have held the slippery prey firmly. Similar teeth can be seen in modern fish-eating animals like crocodiles.

CERESIOSAURUS

NOTHOSAUR FOSSIL

Nothosaur fossils are known from the Alps and from China. Although these animals had legs and toes, their limb bones were not strongly joined to one another and the hips and shoulders were quite weak. This degenerate state shows that they were not well adapted for moving about on land and were better at swimming than walking.

STOMACH STONES

Most good fossilized skeletons of pliosaurs contain collections of gastroliths (stomach stones). Sea-living animals swallow stones to help to adjust their ballast (weight). We find this in animals that swim fast to cach their prey. It is a more versatile system than building up the weight of the skeleton through "pachystosis," a method adopted by the placodonts.

PLIOSAUR TOOTHMARKS

The limb bones of an elasmosaur found in late Jurassic marine rocks in Dorset, England, have given scientists a dramatic clue as to the feeding habits of the pliosaurs. Tooth marks punched deep into the bones match exactly the set of teeth of a big pliosaur. Until this discovery scientists thought that pliosaurs ate only fish and squid.

UNDERWATER ATTACK

From all this evidence we can build up a picture of a late Jurassic marine incident. A long-necked elasmosaur is feeding near the surface. A pliosaur cruises at some depth below, hunting fish and squid. Through the taste of the water it detects the presence of the other reptile. Vomiting out a few stomach stones it adjusts its buoyancy to allow it to rise. Then, when its prey is in view, it "flies" towards it with strong thrusts of its flippers, closing in on a paddle with its mouthful of teeth. Then, having secured a firm hold, the pliosaur twists its massive body, ripping the unfortunate elasmosaur apart before eating it.

TRIASSIC	EARLY/MID JURASSIC	LATE JURASSIC	EARLY CRETACEOUS	LATE CRETACEOUS
245-208 MYA	208-157 MYA	157-146 MYA	146-97 MYA	97-65 MYA

THE GIANTS OF THE SEA

The plesiosaurs were perhaps the most varied group of swimming reptiles during the time of the dinosaurs. They were ocean-going fish-eaters, ranging in size from the length of a small seal to that of a medium-sized whale. They had broad bodies, short tails and two pairs of wing-like paddles with which they flew through the ocean waters. One group had short necks and long heads, while the other had long necks and very small heads. The short-necked types are called the pliosaurs, and the long-necked types the elasmosaurs. The pliosaurs were the larger of the two groups—the sperm whales of the Mesozoic seas.

IN FOR THE KILL

Broad flanges at the back of the skull of a pliosaur must have held massive neck muscles. This suggests that pliosaurs grabbed their larger prey and pulled it to bits with a twisting action. Crocodiles in deep water dismember their food in exactly this way today.

BIG MOUTH

The most spectacular feature of the skeleton of a pliosaur is its huge skull. The long jaws were armed with many sharp teeth, ideal for catching big fish and squid and also for seizing larger prey. The nostrils are surprisingly small and would not have been used for breathing. Instead they would have been used for tasting the water and for judging the speed at which prey was swimming. A pliosaur probably breathed through its mouth when it came to the surface.

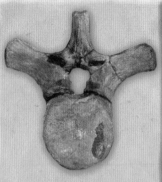

LIOPLEURODON VETEBRAE

This is a vertebrae from *Liopleurodon*, which existed in northern European waters at the end of the Jurassic period. Pliosaurs were an extremely wide-ranging group, with very similar animals existing in Europe at one time, and also at the other side of the world in Australia 80 million years later. It was probably *Liopleurodon* that attacked the elasmosaur in the incident described on page 78.

A RANGE OF PLIOSAURS

We used to think that the pliosaurs were the biggest sea reptiles of all time. Nowadays, however, we are finding the remains of beasts that were even bigger. Nevertheless the biggest of the pliosaurs were very big animals indeed.

There were also many smaller pliosaurs. Their different sizes and head shapes reflected the different lifestyles and the different foods that they were eating. Some must have lived like penguins, darting, and snatching at the weaving and dispersing fish shoals, but the biggest must have been the dolphins and toothed whales of their time. Often all that we know of a particular pliosaur is the skull. As all the bodies were built to a particular well-known plan, scientists assume that we know what the rest of the body was like. Sometimes that gives rise to misconceptions.

MONSTER OF THE DEEP

We used to think that the skull of the pliosaur *Kronosaurus* represented less than a quarter of the length of the whole animal, giving a total length of 40–46 feet (12–14 m)—greater than the contemporary *Tyrannosaurus* on land. More recent studies suggest that the skull was about a third of the total length, making it "just" 26 feet (8 m) long. Still quite a monster!

TRIASSIC	EARLY/MID JURASSIC	LATE JURASSIC	EARLY CRETACEOUS	LATE CRETACEOUS
245-208 MYA	208-157 MYA	157-146 MYA	146-97 MYA	97-65 MYA

A HALF-WAY STAGE

Fossilized bones of sea animals are much more common than those of land animals. They are often found on beaches, where the sea is eroding cliffs of Mesozoic (the era from the Triassic to the Cretaceous) rock, or in quarries where the right kind of rock is being extracted. One of the most complete plesiosaur skeletons ever found was a 16 feet (5 m) long *Rhomaleosaurus*, uncovered in 1851 from stone quarries in Barrow upon Soar, Leicestershire, central England. It was locally known as the "Barrow Kipper" because of the appearance of its spread ribs, and has become the mascot of the village. Scientifically, the odd thing about *Rhomaleosaurus* is the fact that it has a long neck as well as a fairly large head. It is classed as a pliosaur, but it seems to be a part-way stage between the short-necked pliosaurs and the long-necked elasmosaurs.

SUPER-PENGUINS

Dolichorhynchops was a much smaller pliosaur, about 10 feet (3 m) long in total. It lived in the seas that covered late Cretaceous Manitoba in Canada. Judging by its build and its teeth, it swam agilely among the shoals of fish that frequented the waters, snapping them up in its long narrow jaws. It had the same kind of swimming technique as modern penguins, using paddles to get around.

81

UNDERWATER FLIGHT

The plesiosaur paddle worked like a wing. Among the pliosaurs, the strongest muscles pushed the paddles forwards, so this must have been the power stroke. Among the elasmosaurs, there was as much muscle to pull the paddle back as there was to push it forward, allowing the body to turn very quickly. This suggests that the elasmosaurs had much more manoeuvrability than pliosaurs. Nowadays penguins use the same kind of swimming action.

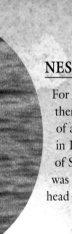

NESSIE

For hundreds of years there have been sightings of an elasmosaur-like creature in Loch Ness, in the Highlands of Scotland. This convincing picture was taken in 1977. But is it a dinosaur's head or a branch?

ARTISTIC IMPRESSIONS

Because of the numerous fossils, the remains of plesiosaurs have been known to fossil collectors for a long time before dinosaurs were discovered. This 19th-century engraving of a prehistoric coastal scene depicts a giant ichthyosaur being attacked by two long-necked plesiosaurs. Although far from perfect, depictions of sea creatures were much more accurate than those of the land-living dinosaurs from the same period.

ELASMOSAURS: THE LONG-NECKS

One early researcher described the long-necked plesiosaurs as "snakes threaded through turtles." Indeed, the broad body and the wing-like flippers are reminiscent of the ocean-going turtle, but the long neck and the little head full of vicious pointed teeth are very different from those of the placid grazing shelled reptile that we know today.

Elasmosaurs were the sea serpents of the time. They existed alongside the pliosaurs in the oceans of the Jurassic and Cretaceous periods.

FLEXIBILITY

The great length of the elasmosaur neck with its huge number of vertebrae have led some to suggest that it would have been as flexible as a snake. But looking at the way the vertebrae are articulated, we can see that this was not quite true.

From side to side there was quite a good degree of movement, but the neck was restricted in the up-and-down plane. Although an elasmosaur could reach downwards with ease, it could not hold its head up like a swan on the surface.

CRYPTOCLIDUS

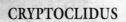

Cryptoclidus was a common elasmosaur found in late Jurassic rocks of Europe. Its mounted skeleton can be seen in several museums. It is typical of the whole elasmosaur group, with its broad body with ribs above and below, its long neck, its mouthful of sharp outward-pointing teeth and its paddles made up of packed bone.

TRIASSIC	EARLY/MID JURASSIC	LATE JURASSIC	EARLY CRETACEOUS	LATE CRETACEOUS
245-208 MYA	208-157 MYA	157-146 MYA	146-97 MYA	97-65 MYA

ELASMOSAUR LIFESTYLE

The elasmosaurs came in all sizes. As time went on there was a tendency for the group to develop longer and longer necks. They probably hunted by ambush. The big body was probably used to disturb shoals of fish, while the little head at the end of the long neck then darted quickly into the group and speared individual fish on the long teeth. Moving the paddles in different directions would have turned the body very quickly into any direction. Their agility meant that they probably hunted near the surface as opposed to the pliosaurs, who were built for sustained cruising at great depths.

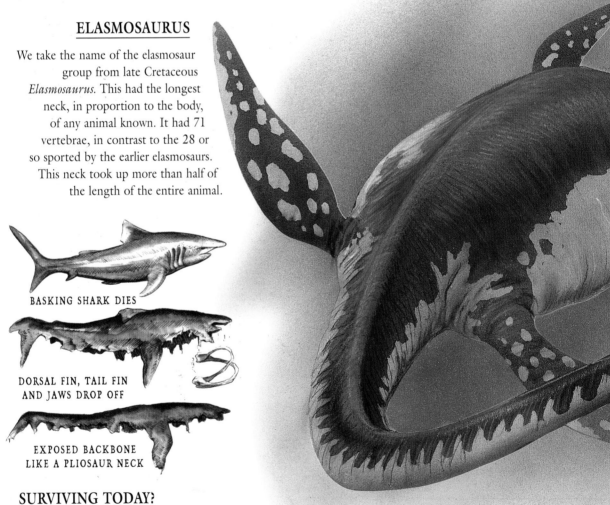

ELASMOSAURUS

We take the name of the elasmosaur group from late Cretaceous *Elasmosaurus*. This had the longest neck, in proportion to the body, of any animal known. It had 71 vertebrae, in contrast to the 28 or so sported by the earlier elasmosaurs. This neck took up more than half of the length of the entire animal.

BASKING SHARK DIES

DORSAL FIN, TAIL FIN
AND JAWS DROP OFF

EXPOSED BACKBONE
LIKE A PLIOSAUR NECK

SURVIVING TODAY?

Now and again we hear stories of people sighting sea serpents that have a distinct similarity to plesiosaurs. Several photographs exist of rotting carcasses with a very plesiosaur look to them. The carcasses usually turn out to be those of basking sharks. Although a basking shark looks nothing like a plesiosaur in life, its dead body deteriorates in a particular pattern. The dorsal fin and the tail fin fall off, losing the shark's distinctive profile. Then the massive jaws drop away. This leaves a tiny brain case at the end of a long string of vertebrae. Instant plesiosaur!

TRIASSIC	EARLY/MID JURASSIC	LATE JURASSIC	EARLY CRETACEOUS	LATE CRETACEOUS
245-208 MYA	208-157 MYA	157-146 MYA	146-97 MYA	97-65 MYA

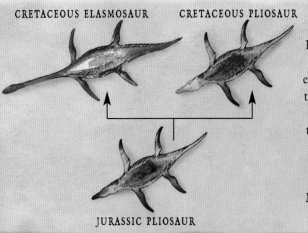

CRETACEOUS ELASMOSAUR CRETACEOUS PLIOSAUR

JURASSIC PLIOSAUR

THE "POLYPHYLETIC" THEORY

It is possible that the elasmosaurs were "polyphyletic"—that means that they did not develop from the one ancestor. The Jurassic elasmosaurs developed from the same ancestors as the nothosaurs of the Triassic period. However, the arrangement of the skull bones of the Cretaceous elasmosaurs has led some scientists to suggest that these later ones actually developed from the short-necked pliosaurs of the Jurassic period. The long neck developed independently in response to environmental pressures—there was food to be had for long-necked animals and so long-necked animals developed. Most scientists, however, believe that all the elasmosaurs developed from the same ancestors—that is, they were "monophyletic."

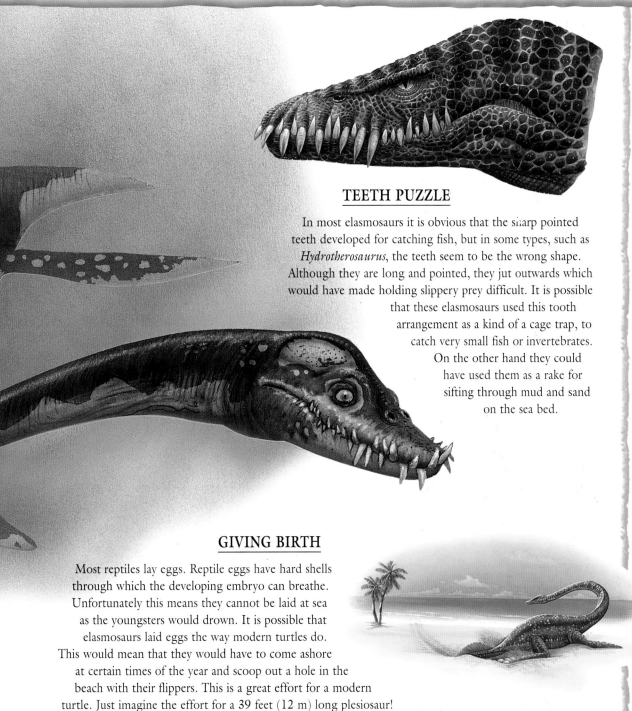

TEETH PUZZLE

In most elasmosaurs it is obvious that the sharp pointed teeth developed for catching fish, but in some types, such as *Hydrotherosaurus*, the teeth seem to be the wrong shape. Although they are long and pointed, they jut outwards which would have made holding slippery prey difficult. It is possible that these elasmosaurs used this tooth arrangement as a kind of a cage trap, to catch very small fish or invertebrates. On the other hand they could have used them as a rake for sifting through mud and sand on the sea bed.

GIVING BIRTH

Most reptiles lay eggs. Reptile eggs have hard shells through which the developing embryo can breathe. Unfortunately this means they cannot be laid at sea as the youngsters would drown. It is possible that elasmosaurs laid eggs the way modern turtles do. This would mean that they would have to come ashore at certain times of the year and scoop out a hole in the beach with their flippers. This is a great effort for a modern turtle. Just imagine the effort for a 39 feet (12 m) long plesiosaur!

A CLEAR IMAGE

Thinly-layered late Jurassic rocks at Holzmaden in Germany are so fine that they contain the impressions of the softest organisms that lived and died there. The bottom of the sea (where the rocks formed) was so stagnant that nothing lived—not even the bacteria that normally break down once-living matter. Among the spectacular fossils found there are the ichthyosaurs, with indications of their soft anatomy still preserved. Flesh and skin still exist as a fine film of the original carbon. For the first time it was obvious that ichthyosaurs had a dorsal fin and a big fish-like fin on the tail. We even have some indication of the color. The carbon in the Holzmaden fossils (above) show that pigment cells were present and would have produced a dark brown tortoiseshell color.

A MODERN RENDERING

Now it is possible to paint an accurate picture of what an ichthyosaur looked like in life. From all the fossils we have found we know that they had streamlined, dolphin-like bodies, with fins on the back and tail. Unlike dolphins the tail fin was not horizontal but vertical. There were two pairs of paddles, the front pair usually bigger than the back pair.

THE ICHTHYOSAUR PIONEER

As with the plesiosaurs, the ichthyosaurs were known before the dinosaurs. Early naturalists, who discovered them in eroding cliffs along the Dorset coast in southern England, mistook them for the remains of ancient crocodiles. Indeed their long jaws and sharp teeth are reminiscent of crocodiles. Mary Anning (1799–1847), a professional fossil collector and dealer from Lyme Regis in Dorset, is credited with finding the first complete fossil ichthyosaur when she was 12 years old. This is a myth, but her collecting and her dealings with the scientists of the day were crucial in furthering our knowledge of these creatures.

ICHTHYOSAURS: THE FISH LIZARDS

Without doubt the most well-adapted marine reptiles of the Mesozoic Era were the ichthyosaurs. If you saw one swimming about you might easily mistake it for a dolphin or even a shark. It is all there—the streamlined body, the triangular fin on the back, the big swimming fin on the tail and the paired swimming organs at the side. Like dolphins, ichthyosaurs were descended from land-living animals and needed to come to the surface to breathe. They developed in Triassic times and shared the Jurassic oceans with the plesiosaurs. They did not survive far into the Cretaceous period, however, and their places were taken by another group of marine reptiles—the mosasaurs—which survived right up until the end of the Mesozoic.

ICHTHYOSAUR SKELETON

Entire skeletons of ichthyosaurs are relatively common, as these creatures were frequently fossilized. Many museums have complete ichthyosaur skeletons on display. This ichthyosaur is in the Bristol City Museum in England.

TRIASSIC 245-208 MYA	EARLY/MID JURASSIC 208-157 MYA	LATE JURASSIC 157-146 MYA	EARLY CRETACEOUS 146-97 MYA	LATE CRETACEOUS 97-65 MYA

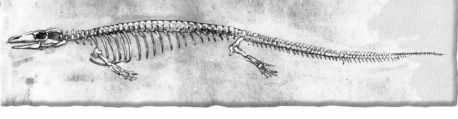

A SWIMMING LIZARD

The aigalosaurs were ancestors of the mosasaurs. They were a group of swimming lizards from the late Jurassic and early to middle Cretaceous periods that lived in Europe. They grew up to 3 feet (1m) long, and had flattened tails but lacked the specialized paddle limbs of their descendants.

DINNER TIME

There is direct evidence that mosasaurs ate ammonites. Ammonites were relatives of modern squid and nautiluses, they sported coiled shells, and were abundant in Cretaceous seas. Consequently, they are also very common as fossils. They lived throughout the Mesozoic in the seas all over the world. One ammonite fossil has been found punctured by toothmarks that exactly match those of a small mosasaur. Evidently the reptile had to bite the ammonite 16 times before crushing the shell and reaching the animal.

FAMILY MEMBER?

The bones of *Mosasaurus* were very similar to those of the modern monitor lizard. Some scientists suspect the two could be distant relatives while others think that the same environmental conditions that lead monitor lizards to develop their distinctive appearance might also have been present in the enviroment *Mosasaurus* inhabited.

GEORGES CUVIER

The jawbones of a completely unknown giant reptile unearthed from the underground quarries near the River Meuse convinced the French anatomist Baron Georges Cuvier (1769–1832) that there were once animals living on the Earth that were completely unlike modern types, and that these ancient animals were periodically wiped out by extinction events.

TRIASSIC 245-208 MYA	EARLY/MID JURASSIC 208-157 MYA	LATE JURASSIC 157-146 MYA	EARLY CRETACEOUS 146-97 MYA	LATE CRETACEOUS 97-65 MYA

MOSASAURS

In 1770, workmen in a chalk quarry near Maastricht in Holland uncovered a long-jawed, toothy skull. Immediately, the owner of the land sued for possession—a circumstance that is all too common in the field of palaeontology even today. Then, in 1794, the French army invaded. Despite the owner's attempt to hide the skull in a cave, it was seized as booty (with the help of a bribe of 600 bottles of wine) and taken back to Paris where it was studied by legendary French anatomist Baron Cuvier. By this time it had been identified as the skull of a huge reptile related to the modern monitor lizards. British geologist William Conybeare gave it the name *Mosasaurus* ("lizard from the Meuse").

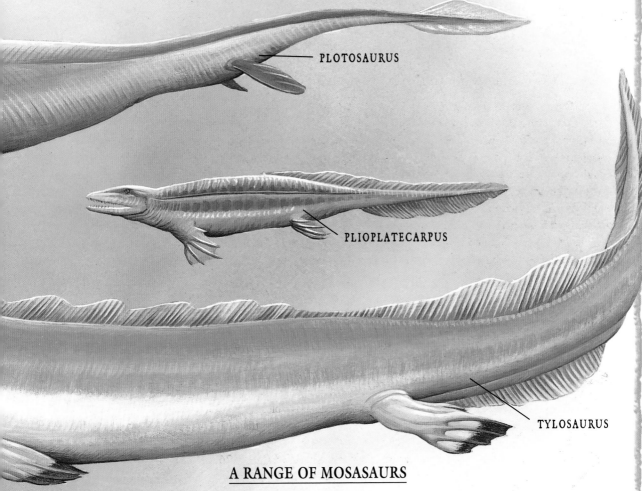

PLOTOSAURUS

PLIOPLATECARPUS

TYLOSAURUS

A RANGE OF MOSASAURS

Mosasaurs are known from late Cretaceous deposits throughout the world. They were all based on a similar body plan and varied in length from 10 feet (3 m) to 33 feet (10 m). Their heads were all very similar to those of the modern monitor lizard and their teeth had adapted to snatch at fish or ammonites. An exception was *Globidens*, which had flattened rounded teeth, which were probably adapted for a shellfish diet.

CROCODILES

Crocodiles have remained essentially unaltered since late Triassic times. However, throughout their history there have been all kinds of specialist types. Some were long-legged and scampered about on land, while some ran about on hind legs like little versions of their relatives, the dinosaurs. More significantly, some developed into sea-living forms showing the same adaptations as other sea-living reptiles—the sinuous bodies, the paddle legs and the finned tails. These were particularly important in Jurassic times.

TELEOSAURUS

METRIORHYNCHUS

GEOSAURUS

A SELECTION OF SEA CROCS

Teleosaurus was a gharial-like sea crocodile. If anything it was even longer and slimmer in build than *Steneosaurus*. *Metriorhynchus* was 10 feet (3 m) long and shows much more extreme adaptations to a sea-going way of life. It lacked the armored scales that we see on more conventional crocodiles. Its legs were converted into paddles that would have been almost useless on land. At the end of its tail the vertebral column was turned downwards, showing that it had a swimming fin like an ichthyosaur. This was a true sea crocodile. *Geosaurus* had the same adaptations as *Metriorhynchus* but appeared somewhat later and, at 7 feet (2 m) long, was considerably smaller. It was much slimmer and the jaws were even narrower.

CHAMPSOSAUR

PHYTOSAUR

CROCODILE

A GOOD SHAPE

Many semi-aquatic meat-eating reptiles have crocodile shapes. The phytosaurs from the late Triassic period could be mistaken for crocodiles except for their nostrils, which were close to the eyes instead of at the tip of the snout. The champsosaurs from the late Cretaceous period of North America were also very crocodile-like, having the same lifestyle in the same habitat. None of these animals was closely related to another and may have developed similar bodies in response to the similar types of environment that they lived in.

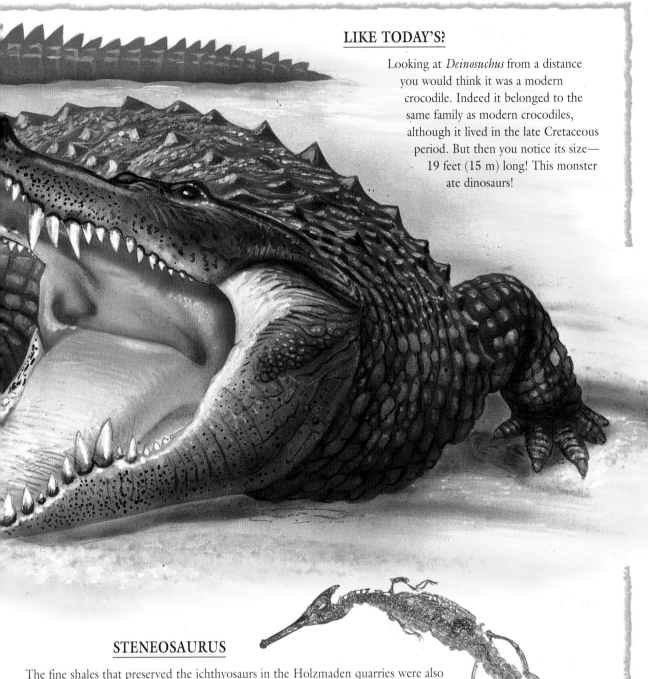

LIKE TODAY'S?

Looking at *Deinosuchus* from a distance you would think it was a modern crocodile. Indeed it belonged to the same family as modern crocodiles, although it lived in the late Cretaceous period. But then you notice its size— 19 feet (15 m) long! This monster ate dinosaurs!

STENEOSAURUS

The fine shales that preserved the ichthyosaurs in the Holzmaden quarries were also very successful in preserving the marine crocodile *Steneosaurus*. We can see that it was very much like a modern crocodile. Its legs and feet show it to have been an animal that spent much of its time on land. However the occurrence of its fossils at Holzmaden and in marine deposits in England show that it was also a sea-going beast. The position of its eyes (on the top of its head) suggests that it attacked shoals of fish from below.

MODERN GHARIAL

In life *Steneosaurus* must have looked very much like the modern gharial of the Indian rivers—the same long narrow jaws with the many sharp fish-catching teeth, the same long body, and tail and the same short legs. However the gharial is a river animal, while *Steneosaurus* hunted in the sea.

TRIASSIC	EARLY/MID JURASSIC	LATE JURASSIC	EARLY CRETACEOUS	LATE CRETACEOUS
245-208 MYA	208-157 MYA	157-146 MYA	146-97 MYA	97-65 MYA

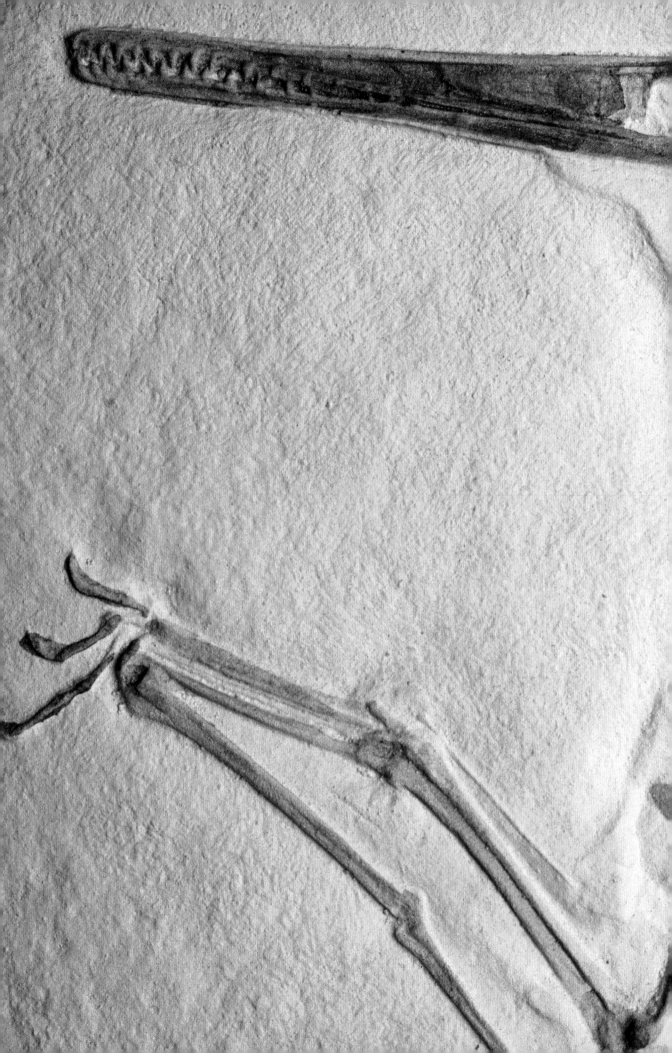

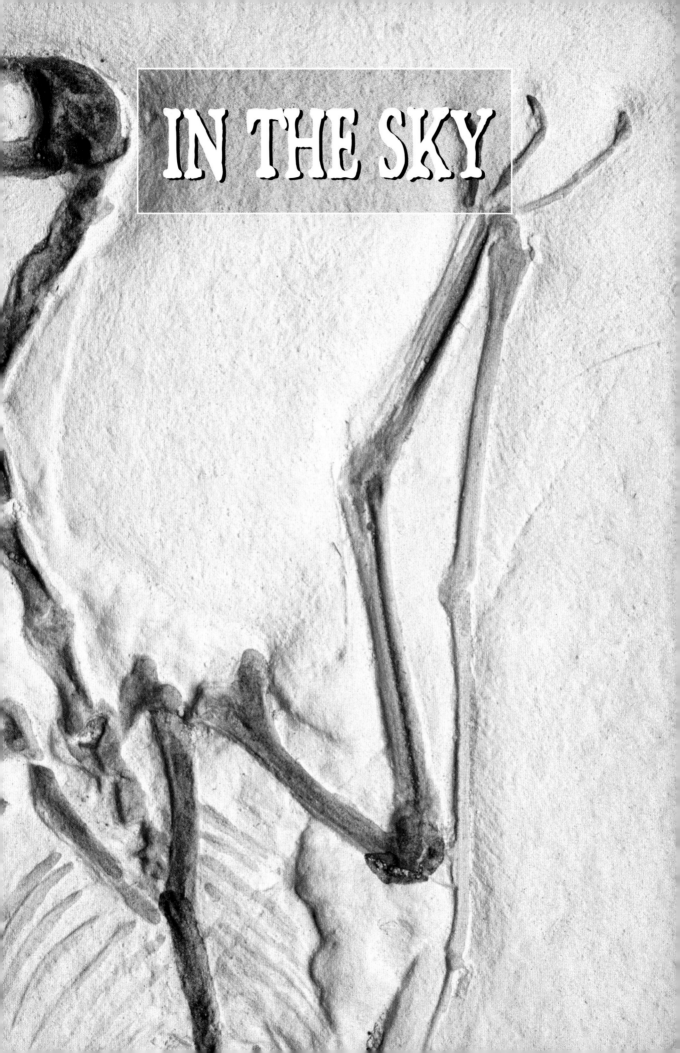

IN THE SKY

WING AND A PRAYER

The earliest flying reptile known was the Permian *Coelurosauravus*. It looked very much like a lizard, but its ribs were extended out to the side and supported gliding wings made of skin. The modern flying lizard of Malaysia glides in exactly the same manner.

KING OF THE SKIES

Gliders like *Coelurosauravus* were replaced in importance by the pterosaurs by late Triassic times. These famous flying reptiles were the first vertebrates to adapt to a life of active flight. They appeared at about the same time as the first dinosaurs, and became extinct at the end of the Cretaceous period. Pterosaur wings were made of reinforced skin stretched out on an arm and an elongated fourth finger.

EARLY BIRDS

Birds such as this *Sinornis* appeared about halfway through the age of dinosaurs, developing from the dinosaurs themselves. Birds continue to thrive, and are the main flying vertebrates today. Their wings are made of a bony structure consisting of some of the fingers fused together, supporting feathers fanning out from the arms.

THE PIONEERS

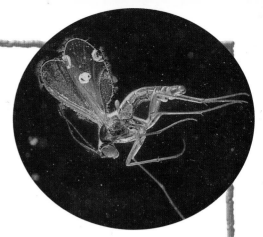

While the dinosaurs, fish, and mammals were colonizing the land and the sea in prehistoric times, the sky up above was buzzing with activity. Early flyers were simple organisms, but nature gradually came up with more complex designs. First came the insects, who continue to flourish today. Next came the flying reptiles, gliding creatures which developed from ground-living, lizard-like animals.

These reptiles were replaced in terms of importance by the pterosaurs, probably the most famous of the ancient flying reptiles. Finally, the first birds appeared halfway through the age of dinosaurs, and have continued to rule the skies to this day.

AMBER PERFECTION

The best fossils come from amber preservation. When an unwary insect gets stuck in the sticky resin that oozes from tree trunks, the resin engulfs the insect and preserves it perfectly. When the tree dies and becomes buried, over a long period of time the resin solidifies and becomes the mineral we call amber. The 1994 film *Jurassic Park* was based on the premise that foreign DNA could be taken from biting insects preserved in amber to recreate the creature that was bitten. While this might not be possible today, it is an exciting concept.

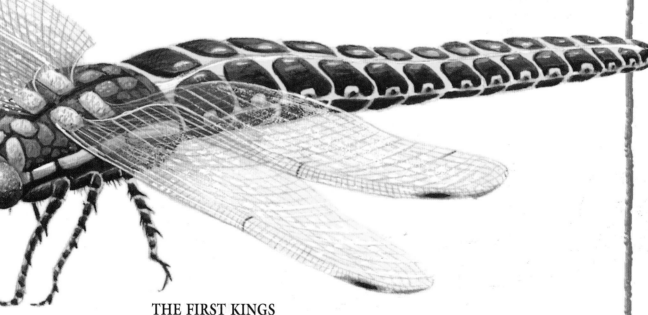

THE FIRST KINGS

Meganeura was like a dragonfly, but much larger—the size of a parrot. Its wings were typical insect wings, consisting of a thin sheet of chitin, supported by a network of rigid veins. *Meganeura* lived in Carboniferous times, not long after insects first developed.

CARBONIFEROUS/PERMIAN	TRIASSIC	EARLY/MID JURASSIC	LATE JURASSIC	EARLY/LATE CRETACEOUS
360-245 MYA	245-208 MYA	208-157 MYA	157-146 MYA	146-65 MYA

SOLAR POWERED

Kuehneosaurus was a gliding reptile
that existed in western England in late Triassic
times. It was very similar in structure to *Icarosaurus*.
There were about a dozen wing supports (about half
the number of the earlier *Coelurosauravus*),
suggesting that the wings were longer and narrower,
and probably more manoeuvrable. The skin of the
wings was probably rich in blood vessels and the
wings may have been able to warm up the
animal in the sun like a solar panel.

LONG LEGS

Late Triassic *Sharovipteryx* from central
Asia was a small lizard-like animal about the
size of a sparrow, with the most ridiculous-
looking hind legs (circled left), each one
longer than the complete length of the body.
These long legs only made sense when it
was noticed that there was the imprint of a
membrane of skin stretched between them
and the middle of the tail.

SHAROVIPTERYX IN FLIGHT

When alive, *Sharovipteryx* must have been able to glide using
the wings on its hind legs. This would not have been a very
stable type of flight, but it was probably efficient enough to
transport the reptile from one tree to another. Small skin
flaps on the forelimbs would have helped to control the flight.
With the wing membrane stretched on elongated limbs,
Sharovipteryx must have resembled a kind of a back-to-front pterosaur.
Indeed it has been suggested that it may have been among the pterosaurs' early relatives.

EARLY FLYING REPTILES

The simplest kind of flight is a gliding flight—one that needs little in the way of muscular effort. All that is required is a lightness of body, and some kind of aerofoil structure that catches the air and allows the body to be carried along upon it, like a paper dart.

In modern times we see this in flying squirrels, flying lizards and even flying frogs. There were a number of flying reptiles in Permian and Triassic times, and each one developed independently from different reptile ancestors.

LONGISQUAMA

This is a fossil of the flying reptile *Longisquama*, from late Triassic central Asia. It had a completely different type of flying mechanism. A double row of long scales stuck up along the backbone, each scale forming a shallow V-shape along its mid line. When spread, these would have overlapped like the feathers of a bird to give a continuous gliding surface. Perhaps they were a precursor to the evolution of feathers in birds, which appeared 60 million years later.

SCALES

A FAMOUS FIND

A famous specimen of late Triassic *Icarosaurus* was discovered by a schoolboy in New Jersey, USA. The partial skeleton shows it to have been a lizard-like animal with long projections from its ribs. The angles at which the rib extensions lay suggested that the wings could have been folded back out of the way when the animal was at rest. Several decades after the discovery, the finder realized that under United States law the specimen was his by rights, and it is now lost to science, having disappeared into his private collection.

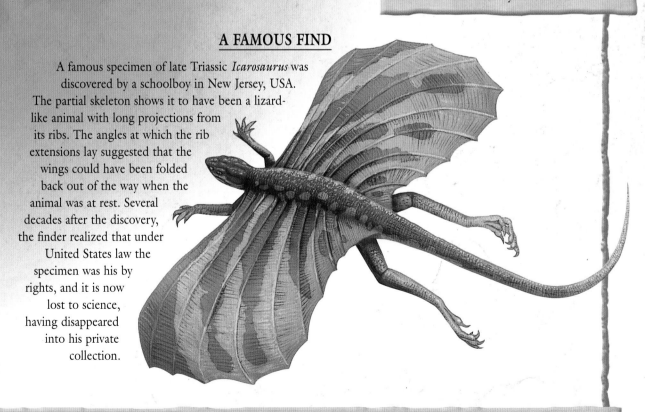

PERMIAN	TRIASSIC	EARLY/MID JURASSIC	LATE JURASSIC	EARLY/LATE CRETACEOUS
286-245 MYA	245-208 MYA	208-157 MYA	157-146 MYA	146-65 MYA

SWIMMING PTEROSAURS

In 1784, the idea was put forward that pterosaurs were not flying animals but swimming animals. This theory influenced many scientists and artists, including Johann Wagler, whose 1830 sketch (left) suggested that pterosaurs were an intermediate stage between mammals and birds.

DEVILISH PTEROSAURS

In 1840 British geologist Thomas Hawkins published a book on the fossil sea reptiles (the ichthyosaurs and plesiosaurs) that had been discovered up to that time. The frontispiece of the book was an engraving by John Martin, an English painter of biblical and historical subjects. It was a nightmare scene in which he depicted monstrous ichthyosaurs and plesiosaurs and pterosaurs that resembled bat-winged demons.

FURRY PTEROSAURS

A surprisingly modern interpretation of pterosaurs was drawn in 1843 by Edward Newman. He regarded them as flying marsupials. Although the mouse ears are inaccurate, the furry bodies and the predatory lifestyle are well in-keeping with how we now regard these creatures.

VICTORIAN TERRORS

The concrete pterosaurs (or "pterodactyles" as they were then called) that were erected in the grounds of the Crystal Palace in south London in 1854 tell us that most Victorians still viewed these creatures as winged dragons. These were more delicate than the surrounding statues of dinosaurs and sea animals, and unfortunately most had been badly damaged or destroyed by the 1930s.

THE DISCOVERY OF THE PTEROSAURS

The first pterosaur fossil to have been scientifically studied was an almost perfect skeleton from the lithographic limestone quarries of Solnhofen in Germany, discovered in 1784. Although the skeleton was just about complete, it was impossible to compare it with any animal alive at the time, so the find remained a mystery. Seventeen years later, the French pioneer naturalist Baron Georges Cuvier guessed that it was a flying animal. Since that date, scientists have come up with many different ideas of what pterosaurs were and how they existed.

JURASSIC BATS?

English geologist Sir Henry De la Beche produced a drawing in 1830 showing animal life in the Jurassic (then called Liassic) sea of southern England. It consisted of swimming reptiles, fish and ammonites, and in the air there were flying pterosaurs. De la Beche depicted pterosaurs as bat-like creatures, with their wing membranes stretching all the way down to their feet.

THE MODERN QUARRIES

The Romans excavated the fine limestone from the Solnhofen quarries to make tiles and paving stones. In the 18th century the fine-grained surface of the rock was found to be ideal for printing, and this led to the rapid expansion of the quarry workings. Despite the fact that these quarries are famous for their fossils (not only of pterosaurs, but of early birds, small dinosaurs, lizards and a whole host of marine animals), it takes the removal of a vast volume of rock to find one worthwhile skeleton.

NORTHERN EUROPE

SHALLOW WATERS (MODERN SOUTHERN GERMANY)

REEF

TETHYS OCEAN

SOLNHOFEN

Over millions of years the surface of the Earth has changed due to the action of plate tectonics, the name given to the activity that occurs under the Earth's surface. Hot magma rises, forcing the Earth to tear on the surface, separating previously joined landmasses. In late Jurassic times the area of southern Germany, including Solnhofen, lay in the shallows along the northern edge of the Tethys Ocean. This ocean separated Europe from Africa. Nowadays all that is left of the Tethys is the Mediterranean Sea and the drying puddles of the Black Sea, the Caspian Sea and the Aral Sea, all flanked by the mountains that were pushed up out of the Earth as the continents collided.

ANATOMY OF A LAGOON

Along the edge of the continental shelf to the north of the Tethys Ocean, a vast reef of sponges grew in the deeper waters. Remains of this reef can now be found stretching from Spain to Romania. As it approached the surface, this reef stopped growing as the sponges died and coral reefs started to grow on top of them. Eventually, a series of lagoons were formed between the reef and the land. Low islands lay across the lagoon, and these (as well as the hinterland) were arid, with only a few scraggly plants. The stagnant water in the lagoon became poisonous and killed any animal that swam or fell into it. Because fine sediment was accumulating below, these animals were preserved almost perfectly.

TRIASSIC 245-208 MYA	EARLY/MID JURASSIC 208-157 MYA	LATE JURASSIC 157-146 MYA	EARLY CRETACEOUS 146-97 MYA	LATE CRETACEOUS 97-65 MYA

SOLNHOFEN: PTEROSAUR PARADISE

Solnhofen in southern Germany has produced a treasure trove of finds—fossils so good that every detail of even the most delicate of organisms can still be seen. The rock is made of very fine particles and was formed under conditions totally lacking in oxygen, so that no further decay was possible. The technical name that geologists give to such occurrences is "lagerstatten." There are only about a dozen such sites known, and most people regard Solnhofen as the best in the world.

THE HEADLESS ONES

Many of the pterosaur fossils found at Solnhofen are without their heads.

The probable reason is that when the pterosaurs died they fell into the shallow waters along the northern edge of the Tethys Ocean.

When the pterosaurs landed, because their bodies were so lightweight they floated at the surface for a while.

While lying on the surface, their floating bodies began to decay and their heads, being the heaviest part, fell off first.

Eventually, after their heads had fallen off, the rest of the pterosaurs' bodies sank to the lagoon floor, where they were quickly covered in fine sediment.

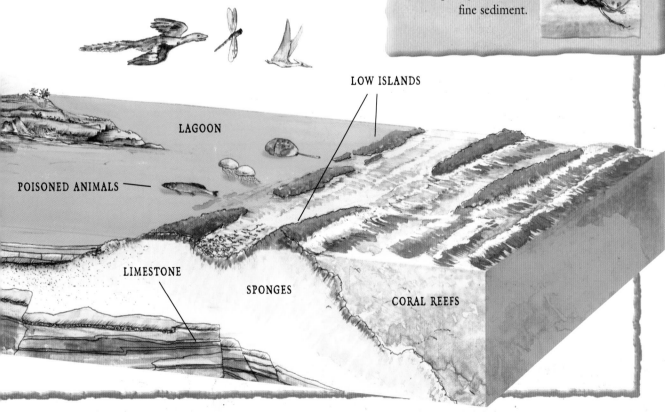

LAGOON

LOW ISLANDS

POISONED ANIMALS

LIMESTONE

SPONGES

CORAL REEFS

NARROW WINGS
PRODUCING ACTIVE,
FLAPPING FLIGHT

THE FANTASY

Many works of fiction, including the film *One Million Years BC*, show pterosaurs carrying away heavy prey like human beings in their feet or their jaws. Even if human beings had been around at that time, the pterosaurs would have been unable to do this without severely disrupting their center of balance.

AN EDUCATED GUESS

Two good fossils of *Eudimorphodon* are known. They both have the wings folded to the body but the wing membrane has not been preserved. Nor is there any direct evidence of a furry pelt. We can, however, guess what the membrane and the fur were like by comparing the fossils with other better preserved pterosaurs.

LONG TAIL

TRIASSIC 245-208 MYA	EARLY/MID JURASSIC 208-157 MYA	LATE JURASSIC 157-146 MYA	EARLY CRETACEOUS 146-97 MYA	LATE CRETACEOUS 97-65 MYA

EUDIMORPHODON

Eudimorphodon had all the physical attributes of the rhamphorhynchoids. It had long, narrow wings made of skin supported by rods of gristle and a wing span of about 3 feet (1 m). Because of its variety of teeth, it could eat many foods, and its furry body facilitated a constantly active lifestyle.

THE EARLIEST PTEROSAUR

The pterosaurs were the most important of the flying animals in Triassic, Jurassic, and Cretaceous times. Once they developed they quickly adopted all the features that were to remain with the group for the rest of their existence. Pterosaurs fall into two groups. The more primitive group—the rhamphorhynchoids—had long tails, short wrist bones and narrow wings. These were the the first to develop, appearing in Triassic times. The other group—the pterodactyloids—developed later, towards the end of the Jurassic period.

SHORT
WRIST
BONES

TEETH OF
DIFFERENT
SIZES

FURRY
BODY

WING MUSCLES

The pterosaurs must have had a flying action like modern bats or birds (right). The arrangement of the shoulder bones and the wing bones show that the muscles present facilitated an active flapping flight.

CATCHING PREY

Many pterosaurs caught fish and, judging by its teeth, *Eudimorphodon* was one of them. The balance of the animal in flight was so delicate that it would not have been able to fly with a fish in its mouth. The pterosaur would have had to have swallowed the fish immediately to get it to its center of balance.

DIMORPHODON SKELETON

The skeletons of *Dimorphodon* fall to pieces and are crushed easily, because they are made up of the finest struts of bone. Nevertheless there have been two good specimens found, and both of these are in the Natural History Museum in London, England.

JURASSIC SKIES

Above the early Jurassic shorelines the air was thick with pterosaurs. They were all of the long-tailed rhamphorhynchoid type. Within a few million years these would all have been replaced by a new pterosaur group—the short-tailed, long-necked, long-wristed pterodactyloids.

BIG HEADS

Rhamphorhynchoid pterosaurs ruled the skies during the early Jurassic period. The earliest Jurassic pterosaur known was discovered in 1828 by the famous professional collector Mary Anning. It was given the name *Dimorphodon* because of its two types of teeth. Scientists today are still in disagreement over many of its features—these disagreements are typical of our lack of knowledge of the pterosaurs in general.

BRILLIANT BEAK

Dimorphodon had two different types of teeth—good for grabbing and holding on to slippery prey such as fish. The skull was very high and narrow, and consisted of windows separated by fine struts of bone. It is very likely that the sides of the head were brightly colored for signaling, just like the beaks of modern tall-beaked birds such as puffins or toucans.

ON THE GROUND

We know that pterosaurs like *Dimorphodon* were very adept at flight, but we are not sure of how they moved around when they were not flying. The old theory was that pterosaurs crawled like lizards, while some scientists saw them as running on their hind legs like birds, with their wings folded out of the way. However, footprints in lake sediments from South America attributed to pterosaurs show the marks of the hind feet walking in a narrow track, with marks seemingly made by the claws of the forelimbs in a wider track on each side. This suggests that pterosaurs were walking upright, using the arms like crutches or walking sticks. A final theory suggests that because of their similarity to bats, maybe they did not come to the ground at all but hung upside down from trees.

TRIASSIC	EARLY/MID JURASSIC	LATE JURASSIC	EARLY CRETACEOUS	LATE CRETACEOUS
245-208 MYA	208-157 MYA	157-146 MYA	146-97 MYA	97-65 MYA

SOFT COVERINGS

Most fossils are of sea-living animals, because sea-living animals have a better chance of falling to the sea bed and eventually becoming entombed in sedimentary rock. However, many pterosaurs lived in coastal areas or around lakes, and fell into the water when they died. Sometimes they were fossilized in environments that preserved the finest of details, such as wing membranes and furry coverings.

WING STRUCTURE

The wing membrane of a pterosaur was stiffened by fine rods of gristle that fanned out from the arm and hand to the wing's trailing edge. The pattern of the gristle stiffening is the same as the arrangement of the flight feathers of a bird, and the supporting fingers of a bat's wing.

A MODERN INTERPRETATION?

It is often thought that birds are the modern equivalent of the pterosaurs. However the modern bat has more in common with the pterosaur than any bird—particularly the membranous wings and the furry covering. Pterosaurs and birds shared the Cretaceous skies, but bats did not develop until pterosaurs died out. This in itself seems to suggest that bats rather than birds occupy the pterosaurs' niche in modern times.

THE BEST PRESERVED

This *Rhamphorhynchus* from the Solnhofen deposits in Germany is one of the best preserved pterosaur fossils we have. Even the structure of its wing membrane is visible.

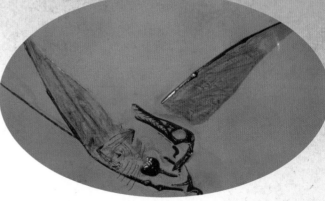

TRIASSIC	EARLY/MID JURASSIC	LATE JURASSIC	EARLY CRETACEOUS	LATE CRETACEOUS
245-208 MYA	208-157 MYA	157-146 MYA	146-97 MYA	97-65 MYA

HOW WERE THE WINGS ATTACHED?

There is a great deal of uncertainty about just how the pterosaur's wings were attached to the animal. Some scientists think that the wings stretched from the arms and fourth finger to the body, and did not touch the hind limbs. Perhaps the wings were attached to the hind limbs at the knee. Alternatively, it is quite possible that the wings stretched right down to the ankle.

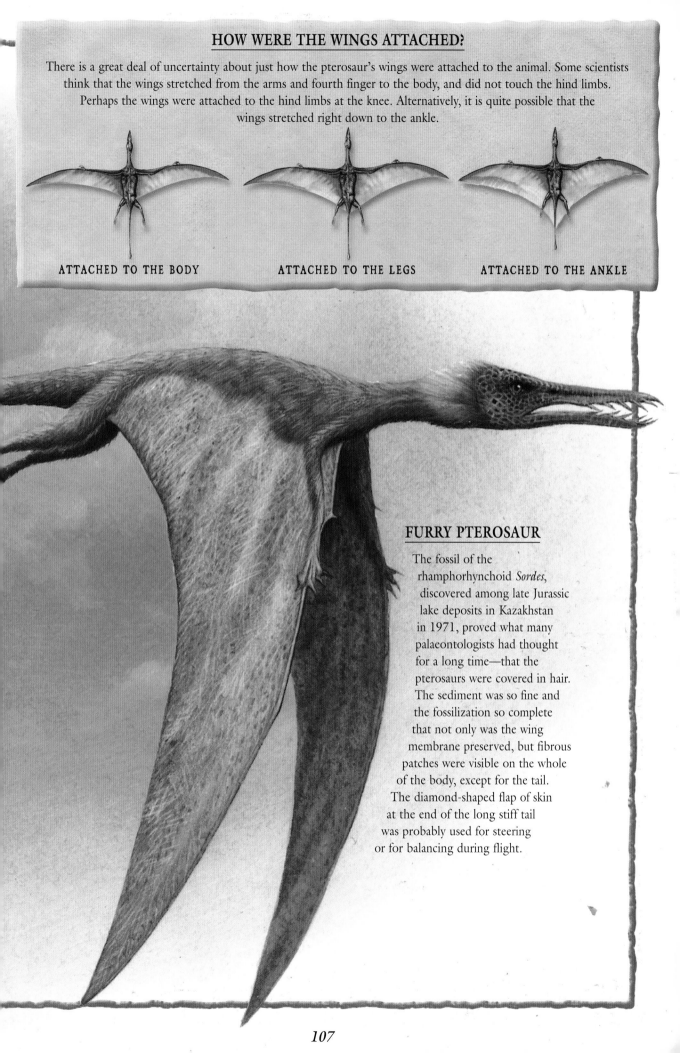

ATTACHED TO THE BODY   ATTACHED TO THE LEGS   ATTACHED TO THE ANKLE

FURRY PTEROSAUR

The fossil of the rhamphorhynchoid *Sordes*, discovered among late Jurassic lake deposits in Kazakhstan in 1971, proved what many palaeontologists had thought for a long time—that the pterosaurs were covered in hair. The sediment was so fine and the fossilization so complete that not only was the wing membrane preserved, but fibrous patches were visible on the whole of the body, except for the tail. The diamond-shaped flap of skin at the end of the long stiff tail was probably used for steering or for balancing during flight.

THEORY OF EVOLUTION

When the British scientist Charles Darwin visited the Galapagos islands in the 19th century, he was struck by the fact that there were a variety of different beak shapes among one family of finch. Their beak shape supported their different lifestyles—heavy beaks for cracking seeds and short beaks for pecking insects and so on. This revelation trigged Darwin's theory of evolution—the idea that over millions of years, creatures could evolve to adapt to their surroundings. The variation in shape of the heads of the various *Pterodactylus* species fits in with Darwin's theory.

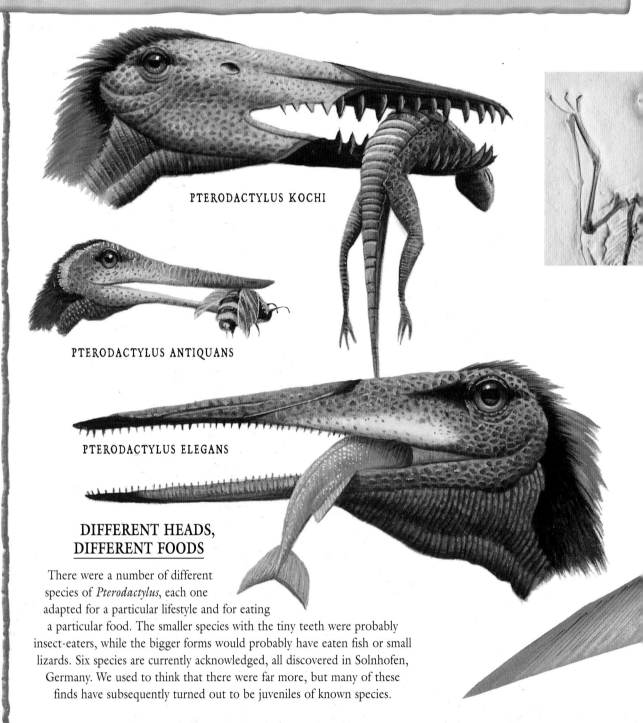

PTERODACTYLUS KOCHI

PTERODACTYLUS ANTIQUANS

PTERODACTYLUS ELEGANS

DIFFERENT HEADS, DIFFERENT FOODS

There were a number of different species of *Pterodactylus*, each one adapted for a particular lifestyle and for eating a particular food. The smaller species with the tiny teeth were probably insect-eaters, while the bigger forms would probably have eaten fish or small lizards. Six species are currently acknowledged, all discovered in Solnhofen, Germany. We used to think that there were far more, but many of these finds have subsequently turned out to be juveniles of known species.

TRIASSIC 245-208 MYA	EARLY/MID JURASSIC 208-157 MYA	LATE JURASSIC 157-146 MYA	EARLY CRETACEOUS 146-97 MYA	LATE CRETACEOUS 97-65 MYA

THE MOST FAMOUS

I t is *Pterodactylus* that gives the pterodactyloid group its name, and indeed pterosaurs are commonly referred to as "pterodactyls." The pterodactyloids dominated in late Jurassic times, but since there are so many different types of pterodactyloid found dating from this time, scientists think their development must have started even earlier.

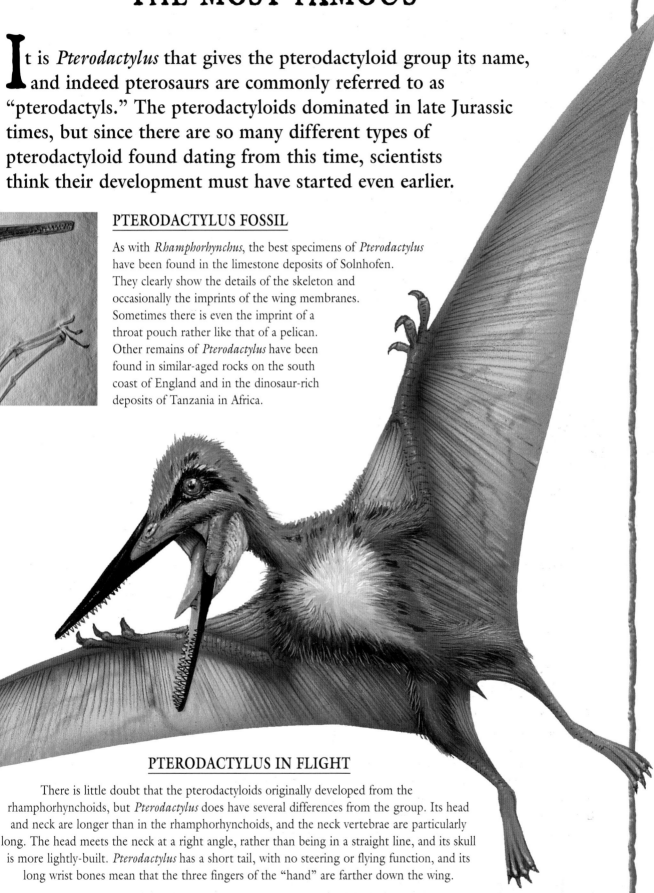

PTERODACTYLUS FOSSIL

As with *Rhamphorhynchus*, the best specimens of *Pterodactylus* have been found in the limestone deposits of Solnhofen. They clearly show the details of the skeleton and occasionally the imprints of the wing membranes. Sometimes there is even the imprint of a throat pouch rather like that of a pelican. Other remains of *Pterodactylus* have been found in similar-aged rocks on the south coast of England and in the dinosaur-rich deposits of Tanzania in Africa.

PTERODACTYLUS IN FLIGHT

There is little doubt that the pterodactyloids originally developed from the rhamphorhynchoids, but *Pterodactylus* does have several differences from the group. Its head and neck are longer than in the rhamphorhynchoids, and the neck vertebrae are particularly long. The head meets the neck at a right angle, rather than being in a straight line, and its skull is more lightly-built. *Pterodactylus* has a short tail, with no steering or flying function, and its long wrist bones mean that the three fingers of the "hand" are farther down the wing.

A QUESTION OF CRESTS

Many pterosaurs had spectacular crests that allowed them to signal to one another and to enable them to identify members of their own species.

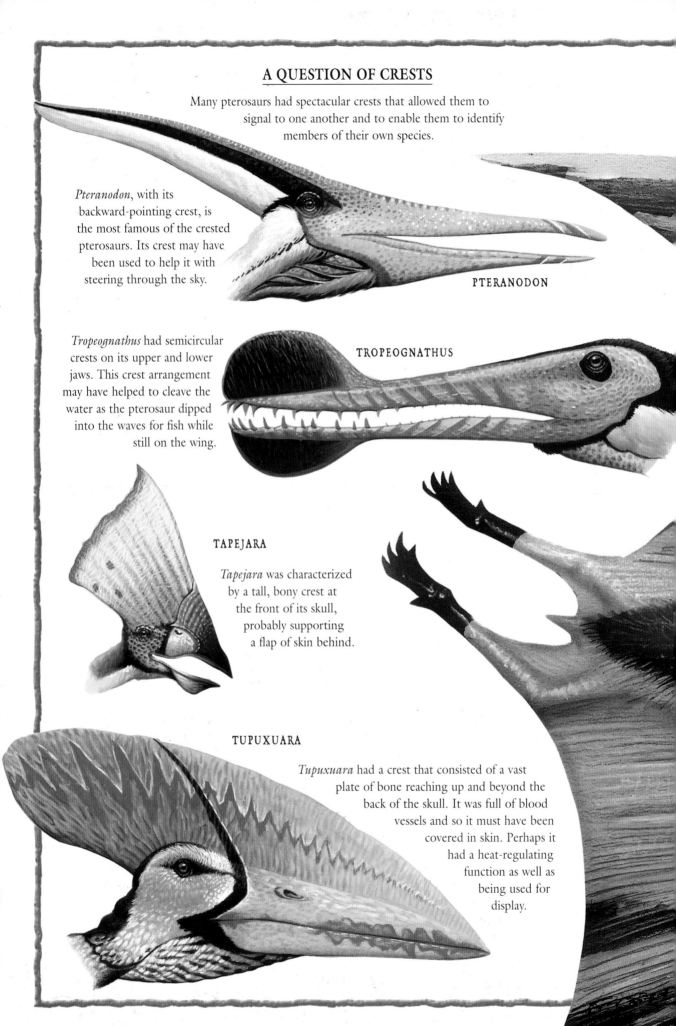

Pteranodon, with its backward-pointing crest, is the most famous of the crested pterosaurs. Its crest may have been used to help it with steering through the sky.

PTERANODON

Tropeognathus had semicircular crests on its upper and lower jaws. This crest arrangement may have helped to cleave the water as the pterosaur dipped into the waves for fish while still on the wing.

TROPEOGNATHUS

TAPEJARA

Tapejara was characterized by a tall, bony crest at the front of its skull, probably supporting a flap of skin behind.

TUPUXUARA

Tupuxuara had a crest that consisted of a vast plate of bone reaching up and beyond the back of the skull. It was full of blood vessels and so it must have been covered in skin. Perhaps it had a heat-regulating function as well as being used for display.

HEADS & CRESTS

There are birds of every kind today, ranging from perching birds and swimming birds to wading birds and hunting birds. Modern birds have a variety of different heads and beaks—deep, strong beaks for cracking nuts; long, pointed beaks for probing mud; short, sharp beaks for pecking insects; and hooked beaks for tearing flesh. This variety was just as pronounced among the pterodactyloids. As the age of reptiles continued, they diversified into all different types, and had different head shapes to suit their different lifestyles.

HIDEOUS FIND

One of the most grotesque of the pterosaurs was *Dsungaripterus*. It had a beak like a pair of upturned forceps, a battery of crushing, tooth-like, bony knobs at the back of the jaws and a crest that stretched from the back of the head to the snout. It was a large pterosaur with a wingspan of over 10 feet (3 m). *Dsungaripterus* was the first pterosaur to be discovered in China.

DSUNGARIPTERUS RESTORED

We can usually tell how an animal lived and what it ate by looking at its jaws. *Dsungaripterus*, from the early Cretaceous period, probably ate shellfish. The narrow pointed jaws could have been used for extracting shellfish from rocky crannies, and the shells would have been crushed by the tooth-like knobs in the back of their jaws. The crest was probably brightly colored and might have been used for signaling to other pterosaurs.

TRIASSIC	EARLY/MID JURASSIC	LATE JURASSIC	EARLY CRETACEOUS	LATE CRETACEOUS
245-208 MYA	208-157 MYA	157-146 MYA	146-97 MYA	97-65 MYA

PTERANODON SKELETON

This partial skeleton of the giant pterosaur *Pteranodon* was found in Cretaceous rocks in Kansas, USA. It shows a skull fragment, the bones of the wing finger, and the complete hind legs. The whole skeleton was extremely lightweight, and the bones had openings to allow the penetration of air sacks, connected to the lungs. A similar system is also seen in modern birds.

QUETZALCOATLUS

PTERANODON

ARGENTAVIS

A FLIGHT OF MONSTERS

Pteranodon has the perception of being the largest of the pterosaurs. The biggest species of *Pteranodon* had a wingspan of about 30 feet (9 m). However, in the 1970s remains from an even larger pterosaur were found in late Cretaceous rocks in Texas. It was given the name *Quetzalcoatlus*, after the flying serpent from Aztec mythology. All sorts of different estimates were made about the size of this beast. The current estimate is that it had a wingspan of about 36–39 feet (11–12 m). The biggest bird known is the condor-like *Argentavis* from Argentina, which existed around 35 million years ago. It had a wingspan of 25 feet (7 m). Among living birds, the royal albatross has the biggest wingspan, reaching 10 feet (3 m).

THE BIGGEST

Peranodon was discovered in the 1870s in the late Cretaceous beds of Kansas in the United States. It had a wingspan of over 30 feet (9 m). Scientists were astounded, since this was before the development of powered aviation and nobody had really experimented with the sizes of flying structures. Now it looks pretty modest when compared with some more recent discoveries.

THE BIGGEST—FOR THE MOMENT

While the Quetzalcoatlus is widely considered to be the largest flying animal of all time, the wingspan of the *Arambourgiana* has also been estimated at around 39 feet (12 m). As this estimate was based on just one bone the debate continues. The *Arambourgiana* was a pterodactyloid and had an extremely long neck. When the neck bones were first found they were thought to have been the long finger bones that supported the wing. The original name given to it was *Titanopteryx*, but that name had already been given to something else, so the title had to be changed.

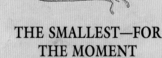

THE SMALLEST—FOR THE MOMENT

Until recently the tiny *Anurognathus* held the record for the smallest pterosaur with a wingspan of about 2 feet (50 cm). In 2008 however, a new species of pterosaur was discovered in China. With a wingspan of just 1 foot (25 cm) it was about the size of a modern sparrow. The fossil was found in an ancient waterway in northwestern China and shows that the pterosaur was toothless. Its curved feet suggest that it lived in trees.

TRIASSIC	EARLY/MID JURASSIC	LATE JURASSIC	EARLY CRETACEOUS	LATE CRETACEOUS
245-208 MYA	208-157 MYA	157-146 MYA	146-97 MYA	97-65 MYA

THE FIRST BIRD

FEATHER

The first *Archaeopteryx* fossil to be found was just the feather. In isolation it looks like nothing unusual. It is a perfectly conventional flight feather as could be found on a modern bird. The main support is a vane that is off-center, showing that it is from a wing and used for flight. The filaments forming the vane of the feather had rows of hooks that enabled them to fix to one another to give stability—just as in a modern bird. There was a downy portion at the base for insulation, as modern birds have. It was discovered just a year before the first partial skeleton was found.

I n 1859 Charles Darwin published *The Origin of Species,* creating an immediate row. Many people, and some scientists, found it difficult to believe that animals had evolved into different types over a long period. Then, two years later, a remarkable fossil was discovered in the quarries of Solnhofen in Germany. It seemed to be a dinosaur, but it sported a bird's wings and was covered in feathers. Here were the remains of a creature that appeared to be a stage in the evolution of birds from dinosaurs. Some saw it as proof of Darwin's theories while others thought the fossil was a hoax. Even today, the fossil of *Archaeopteryx* (as this creature was named) still prompts a lot of debate both among people who agree and disagree with Darwin.

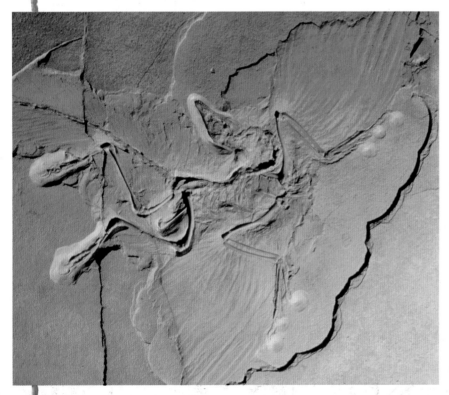

VINDICATING DARWIN ?

Eight *Archaeopteryx* fossils have been found so far, all from the Solnhofen quarries, ranging in quality from a single feather to an almost complete bony skeleton with feathers. One was found in a private collection, having been misidentified as the small dinosaur *Compsognathus.* This specimen did not show the feathers, and the misidentification serves to emphasize the resemblance between the primitive bird and the dinosaur ancestor.

THE LIVING ARCHAEOPTERYX

Had we seen *Archaeopteryx* in life, fluttering away from us, there would be no doubt in our minds that we were looking at a bird, albeit a rather clumsy one. However, a closer look would reveal a set of toothed jaws, just like a dinosaur, instead of the usual bird beak. The tail appeared to be paddle-shaped, unlike a modern bird's muscular stump with a bunch of feathers. This tail was a stiff straight rod, like a dinosaur's tail, with feathers growing from each side. The final oddity would be the claws, three of them protruding from the leading edge of the wing. Just as the fossils suggest, a living *Archaeopteryx* would likely have appeared part bird and part dinosaur.

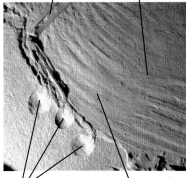

COVERTS   PRIMARIES

CLAWS   SECONDARIES

THE WING

The wing of *Archaeopteryx* was no halfway measure. Apart from the clawed fingers it was identical in structure to the wing of a modern flying bird, with the elongated finger-like primary feathers, bunched secondaries and coverts streamlining the whole structure. The wing muscles would have been weaker than those of a modern bird as there was no strong keeled breastbone to anchor them, but the flying action must have been the same.

TRIASSIC 245-208 MYA	EARLY/MID JURASSIC 208-157 MYA	LATE JURASSIC 157-146 MYA	EARLY CRETACEOUS 146-97 MYA	LATE CRETACEOUS 97-65 MYA

CAUDIPTERYX'S ENVIRONMENT

Caudipteryx (foreground), part of the Chinese "Gang of Three," lived in an environment like the one shown above. Forests of conifers and ginkgoes, with an undergrowth of ferns and cycads, provided refuge and food for all sorts of different animals in late Jurassic and early Cretaceous China. Lizards and small mammals scampered through the undergrowth and little feathered theropod dinosaurs hunted between the trees. The air was colonized by birds (some looking like modern types), while on the ground raced several different half-dinosaur, half-bird creatures.

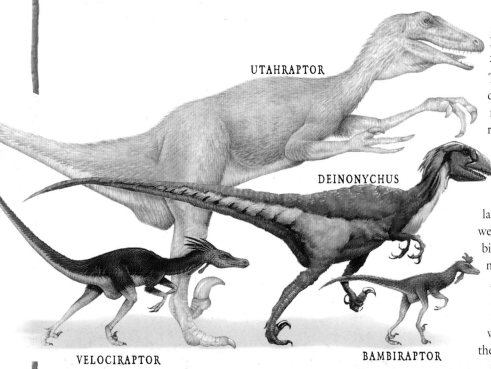

UTAHRAPTOR

DEINONYCHUS

VELOCIRAPTOR

BAMBIRAPTOR

MANIRAPTORAN DINOSAURS

The group of meat-eating dinosaurs known as the maniraptorans have always been recognized as being very bird-like animals. Attempts have been made to put them on the ancestral tree of the birds, but the problem is that, being late Cretaceous dinosaurs, they were much later than the first bird *Archaeopteryx*. Perhaps the maniraptorans developed from *Archaeopteryx*, or *Archaeopteryx*-like birds that lost their powers of flight. If that were the case, they would have been very much like the Chinese "Gang of Three."

CHINESE "GANG OF THREE"

Across the contemporary European-Asian landmass, where China's Liaoning province now lies, a series of forest-shrouded inland lakes produced fossils that were just as spectactular as those from Solnhofen. These include three kinds of animal that, like *Archaeopteryx*, show the evolutionary connection between birds and dinosaurs. Only recently, with improved scientific exchanges between China and the West, is their true significance being fully appreciated.

SINOSAURIPTERYX

One of the little dinosaurs present in the Liaoning province was *Sinosauropteryx*. It seems to have been covered in fur or feathers. The preservation is so good that a kind of downy fuzz is visible all around the bones. Although there is still some dissent, most scientists are convinced that this represents a covering of "protofeathers," structures that are part way between hair, like that of a mammal, and feathers, like those of a bird.

SINOSAUROPTERYX FOSSIL

Only the downy covering on this skeleton shows *Sinosauropteryx* to have been related to the birds. Apart from that, it appears to be a meat-eating dinosaur. The long legs and tail show it to have been a swift-running animal, while the short arms came with three claws. Three skeletons of *Sinosauropteryx* have been found, and their stomach contents show that they hunted lizards and small mammals that existed at that time.

HALF-BIRD, HALF-DINOSAUR

Another small animal was *Protarchaeoteryx*. It was about the same size as *Sinosauropteryx* but it had a short tail and much longer arms. It was also covered in fuzz and, although the only skeleton found was very jumbled up, there seemed to be long feathers along the arms and tail. The feathers on the arms would have given a wing-like structure, but it would not have been sufficent to give the animal any power of flight.

TRIASSIC 245-208 MYA	EARLY/MID JURASSIC 208-157 MYA	LATE JURASSIC 157-146 MYA	EARLY CRETACEOUS 146-97 MYA	LATE CRETACEOUS 97-65 MYA

THE FIRST BEAK

Confuciusornis is the first beaked bird that we know of. A beak is a much more practical, lightweight alternative to the heavy teeth and jaws of a reptile. It consists of a sliver of bone, sheathed in a lightweight horny substance that combines strength with lightness. Anything that reduces their weight is an advantage to a flying animal.

ALULA

FLIGHT CONTROL

Eoalulavis from early Cretaceous lake deposits in Spain is the first bird that we know to have carried an alula. This is a tuft of feathers on the leading edge of the wing, more-or-less where our thumb is. With very small movements of this structure the passage of air over the wing can be altered considerably, and this makes the flight much more controllable. All modern birds have this. However, fossils of *Eoalulavis* are unclear about whether or not the bird had other advanced features such as a beak.

CONFUCIUSORNIS FOSSIL

Many hundreds of fossils of *Confuciusornis* have been uncovered at the Liaoning site in China. Some are so well preserved that the details of the plumage are clear. Some have long tail feathers, like those of a bird of paradise, while others have none. This suggests that, as in modern birds, the males had much more flamboyant plumage than the females.

TRIASSIC 245-208 MYA	EARLY/MID JURASSIC 208-157 MYA	LATE JURASSIC 157-146 MYA	EARLY CRETACEOUS 146-97 MYA	LATE CRETACEOUS 97-65 MYA

TOWARDS MODERN BIRDS

For all its fine feathers, *Archaeopteryx* was still mostly dinosaur. It had a long reptilian tail, fingers on the wings and a jaw full of teeth. Modern birds have stumpy tails called pygostyles, supporting long feathers. Their wing fingers have completely disappeared, and they also have beaks instead of jaws and teeth. These are all weight-saving adaptations, that developed as a means of making the bird as light as possible so that it can fly more efficiently. These features seem to have appeared at different times during the age of dinosaurs.

A MODERN TAIL

Iberomesornis, a fossil bird from early Cretaceous rocks in Spain, is the earliest bird known to have a pygostyle tail. This structure consists of a muscular stump from which the tail feathers grow in a fan arrangement. The muscles of the pygostyle can spread the tail feathers out or bunch them together, helping to control flight or make a display for courting purposes.

THE PERCHING FOOT

Birds that live in trees usually have feet in which the first toe is turned backwards, enabling the foot to grasp a small branch so the bird can perch. An early example of a perching foot is found in *Changchengornis*—a close relative of *Confuciusornis*—also found in the Liaoning rocks in China. This bird also had a hooked beak, suggesting that it was a meat-eater like a hawk.

Hesperornis was a swimming bird of late Cretaceous North America. As big as a man, it must have looked something like a penguin, but with no forelimbs at all, and a long beak full of teeth. This leg bone was found in the chalk deposits in West Kansas, United States.

BIRDS THAT LIVED LIKE DINOSAURS

Once the dinosaurs died out, a number of huge, flightless hunting birds developed around 65 million years ago. *Phorusrhachos* of South America and *Diatryma* of North America were built along the lines of medium-sized meat-eating dinosaurs, with fast hind legs and fierce heads. *Titanis* (above) from Florida even had tiny clawed hands on the remains of its wings. It is almost as if there had still been a niche for dinosaur-shaped hunting creatures and giant hunting birds had developed to filled it.

KILLER DUCK

Bullockornis lived in Australia around 20 million years ago. It stood 10 feet (3 m) high and had a huge beak that was either used for cracking nuts or tearing flesh. An enlarged brain capacity suggests that the latter was more likely, as quick senses are necessary for hunting down prey. It was unrelated to the emus or the cassowaries, or any other type of flightless bird that exists in Australia today. Despite its dinosaur-like appearance, *Bullockornis* was actually a kind of a duck.

ABANDONING FLIGHT

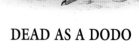

Wh
hile many birds developed the ability to fly, some birds seem to have developed the ability and abandoned it soon after. There are several possible explanations for why this might happen. Perhaps flightless birds developed in areas where there were no dangerous predators on the ground and so there was no need to fly, or perhaps food was more plentiful on the ground.

DEAD AS A DODO

Probably the best known of the extinct flightless birds is *Raphus*, the dodo. It developed from pigeon stock into a ground-dwelling plant-eater on the island of Mauritius. It survived there happily for thousands of years, as there were no ground-living predators. Everything changed, however, when humans arrived on the island, and the bird was wiped out within a few years.

PLANT-EATERS

Not only were the shapes of the meat-eating dinosaurs reflected in some of the later birds, but there seemed to be bird versions of the long-necked plant-eaters as well. *Dinorinis*, the moa, existed in New Zealand right up until modern times. It thrived there because there were no ground-living predators in New Zealand—until human beings came along and caused its extinction.

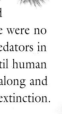

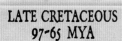

LATE CRETACEOUS 97-65 MYA	PALEOGENE 65-23 MYA	NEOGENE 23-1.8 MYA	QUATERNARY 1.8-0.01 MYA

SINCE THE DINOSAURS

The end of the Cretaceous period was marked by a mass extinction. However, the birds lost only three quarters of their species and the remainder soon re-established themselves as the masters of the skies. As the mammals spread in the absence of dinosaurs, so they took to the skies as well. The bats developed as a successful group, and other mammal groups developed gliding forms. There were even gliding reptiles and amphibians. Throughout all this, the insects continued to buzz, as they have done since Carboniferous times.

THE WEBBED WAY

The birds that survived the mass extinction went on to become the true masters of the skies. The birds of today mostly fly, but they can also perch, wade, swim, and even burrow. *Presbyornis* was a long-legged wading duck that lived in huge flocks in North America around 65 million years ago. Although it had webbed feet, its legs would have been too long to allow it to swim. The webs probably developed to prevent it from sinking into the mud.

THE TRUE KINGS

Insects appeared nearly 400 million years ago, and immediately developed flying types. Few died out in the end-Cretaceous mass extinction, and they are now far more diverse than any other group of creatures. Wings are the tough parts of an insect's anatomy, and it is mostly wings that have been fossilized. Occasionally the preservation is so good that the patterns and markings are preserved, although the colors are not recorded.

LATE CRETACEOUS 97-65 MYA	PALEOGENE 65-23 MYA	NEOGENE 23-1.8 MYA	QUATERNARY 1.8-0.01 MYA

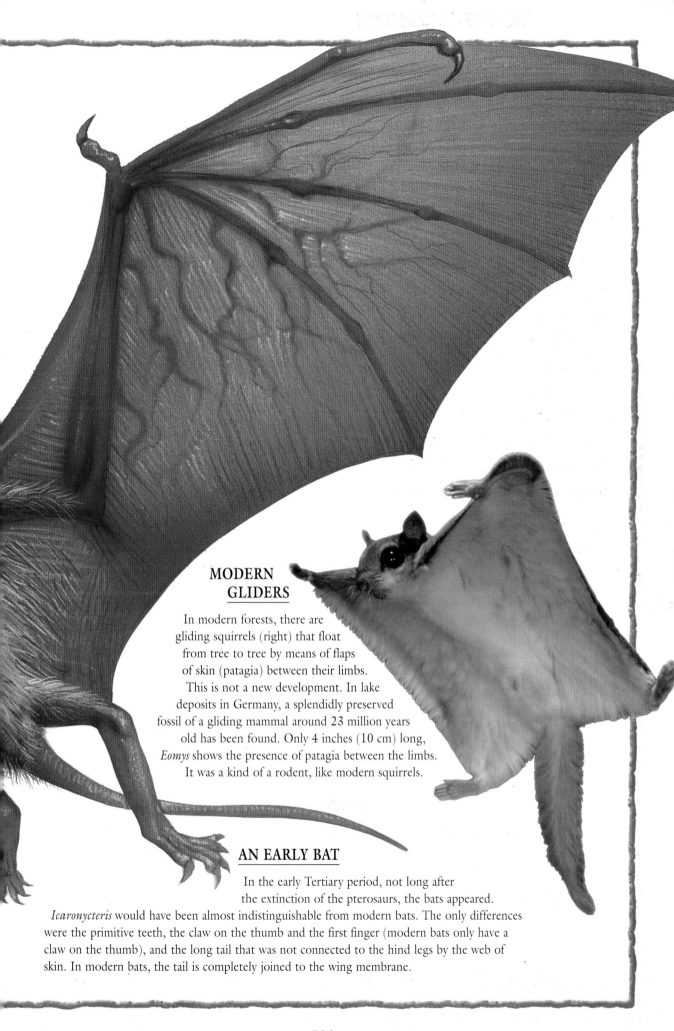

MODERN GLIDERS

In modern forests, there are
gliding squirrels (right) that float
from tree to tree by means of flaps
of skin (patagia) between their limbs.
This is not a new development. In lake
deposits in Germany, a splendidly preserved
fossil of a gliding mammal around 23 million years
old has been found. Only 4 inches (10 cm) long,
Eomys shows the presence of patagia between the limbs.
It was a kind of a rodent, like modern squirrels.

AN EARLY BAT

In the early Tertiary period, not long after
the extinction of the pterosaurs, the bats appeared.
Icaronycteris would have been almost indistinguishable from modern bats. The only differences
were the primitive teeth, the claw on the thumb and the first finger (modern bats only have a
claw on the thumb), and the long tail that was not connected to the hind legs by the web of
skin. In modern bats, the tail is completely joined to the wing membrane.

INDEX

ACKNOWLEDGEMENTS

We would like to thank: Helen Wire, www.fossilfinds.com and Elizabeth Wiggans for their assistance.
Illustrations by John Alston, Lisa Alderson, Dougal Dixon, Simon Mendez and Luis Rey.

North American edition copyright © 2009 *ticktock* Entertainment Ltd.
First published in North America by *ticktock* Media Ltd., The Old Sawmill, 103 Goods Station Road, Tunbridge Wells, Kent, TN1 2DP, UK.

ISBN 978 1 84696 988 1 (paperback).
Printed in China   10 9 8 7 6 5 4 3 2 1

Picture Credits:
(t=top, b=bottom, c=center, l=left, r=right, OFC=outside front cover, IFC=inside front cover, IBC=inside back cover, OBC=outside back cover)
A-Z Botanical: 52bl, 53tr, 59cr. Lisa Alderson: IFC, 8bl, 8-9c, 16-17c, 23t, 26l, 27c, 31c, 35br, 45br, 48b, 49b, 50b, 58-59c, 62-63c, 71b,
72-73cl, 81t, 82-83c, 90c, 96b, 105b, 106-107c, 112l, 116b, 117t, 121bl. John Alston: 8tl, 12-13c, 13t, 18t, 18b, 20tl, 21t, 24cl, 24bl,
27tr, 30tl, 30bl, 31tr, 32tl, 39tl, 39tr, 39b, 43cr, 44t, 52b, 54t, 55c, 61t, 65t, 66t, 70b, 72l, 73r, 74b, 75r, 77t, 82t, 84l, 85t, 88t, 100
cl, 101b, 101tr, 103c, 103bl, 103br, 107t, OBCtr, OBCbr. BBC Natural History Unit: 62b, 66b, 71tr, 75t, 76tl, 79cr, 88c, 91b, 106cl.
Dr. Jose Bonaparte: 39t. Corbis: 5t, 12tl, 15b, 26b, 27tr, 29cr, 29br, 30cb, 77b, 88bl, 92-93, 100t, 106b, 108cr. Dougal Dixon: 9b, 11b,
14b, 15tl, 15tr, 23b, 35tr. Steve Etches: 78tl. Fossil Finds: 8cl, 18c, 33br, 41t, 47t, 64cl, 65b, 72b, 86t, 88cl. Dr. Peter Griffiths: 6-7, 19t,
23, 99c, 110b. Humboldt Museum: 44cl. Simon Mendez: OFC, 3, 4b, 5t, 12t, 13b, 14c, 16-17c, 20-21c, 21b, 22b, 22-23c, 24tl, 28-29c,
33cr, 34c, 38-39c, 40t, 40-41c, 42-43c, 44-45b, 46b, 50-51c, 54-55c, 56-57c, 60-61c, 62t, 66-67c, 70c, 74-75c, 76-77c, 80-81c, 85cr,
85br, 88-89c, 90bl, 94-95, 96-97c, 104c, 105t, 108c, 110t, 117t, 118t, 119t, 119b, 120c, 122cl. Museum of Utah: 60tl, OBCtl, OBCbr.
National Museum of Wales: 99c, 110b. National Trust: 43cl. Bob Nicholls: 78-79c. Oxford City Museum: 10tl, 10c, 10tr. Paleontologisk
museum, Oslo: 96cl, 97cr, 118b. Peterborough Museum: 79b. Planet Earth Pictures: 16bl. Luis Rey: 2, 5b, 25c, 32-33c,
46t, 47c, 52-53c, 66cl, 74t, 84-85c, 90-91c, 97b, 102cl, 109c, 111c, 112-113c, 115c, 120cl, 122-123c. Science Photo Library: 82b.
Paul Sereno: 4t, 9cr, 34tr. Professor Kent Stephens: 43t. University of Bristol: 87b. University of Toronto: 70tr.
Every effort has been made to trace the copyright holders and we apologize in advance for any unintentional omissions. We would be pleased
to insert the appropriate acknowledgement in any subsequent edition of this publication.